Poems to Lift You Up
&
Make You Smile

Compiled by

Jayne Jaudon Ferrer

Parson's Porch Books

Poems to Lift You Up & Make You Smile
ISBN: Softcover 978-1-955581-09-7
Copyright © 2021 by Jayne Jaudon Ferrer

Parson's Porch Books is an imprint of Parson's Porch *&* Company (PP*&*C) in Cleveland, Tennessee. PP*&*C is an innovative organization which raises money by publishing books of noted authors, representing all genres. Its face and voice is **David Russell Tullock** (dtullock@parsonsporch.com).

Parson's Porch *&* Company *turns books into bread & milk* by sharing its profits with the poor.

www.parsonsporch.com

Poems to Lift You Up
&
Make You Smile

*For anyone who needs a reminder that every day is a gift
and that, even in our darkest hours,
there are always blessings to be found.*

Acknowledgments

Your Daily Poem launched in June 2009 with a single goal: to share the pleasure of poetry with those who may not have had the opportunity to develop an appreciation for that genre—usually due to a boring experience in a classroom. Over the last 12 years, I've had the privilege of sharing poetry that is anything *but* boring. Along the way, a second goal emerged: to provide a daily dose of something positive and uplifting. This book is a harvest of "the cream of the crop"—100 poems selected out of the nearly 4000 archived on YDP for their ability to make you smile.

I am so grateful to the poets whose wonderful words are included in this book, and to those who have allowed me to showcase their work on YourDailyPoem.com. I'm also grateful to Dan and Rene' Batson for their friendship and for introducing me to Parson's Porch; to David Russell Tullock and his team for turning this anthology into a reality; to my precious family for their constant encouragement of my sundry writing projects, and to YDP subscribers around the world—most of who never suspected when they signed up that, more than a decade later, they'd still be reading a poem every day!

Jayne Jaudon Ferrer
Editor, YourDailyPoem.com

Table of Contents

Poems to Lift You Up

Our True Song
by
Kevin Arnold

Our simple acts may be the warp and weft
Of the substance of our lives, what is left

Beyond the gifts and wills, the trusts and estates
After our *belles lettres* or *plein air* landscapes

What if our day-to-day actions, in the long slog
Of life are our lasting legacy, our true song?

Kevin Arnold holds an MFA in Creative Writing from San Jose State
University. Author of a novel, *The Sureness of Horses*, and a poetry collection,
Nineteen Poems Around a Divorce and Beyond, he enjoys skiing, playing
competitive tennis and duplicate bridge, and is working on a second novel
and another collection of poems. Learn more about Kevin
at www.kevinarnoldauthor.com.

The Doe
by
Susan B. Auld

Her face peered at me through tall grass
and we held our breath,
still-lives in dappled light,
not sure of the other
curious-wonder at meeting at all.

I spoke calming
she listened

I stepped passing
she stood still.

We held each other with our eyes,
slow danced at the edge of the golden woods
on an orange October morning.

The moon and sun watched
as the south wind brushed past the north
to warm the day,
midnight frost trickled
sliding off the brittle leaves swirling.

I moved away.
I felt her follow.

And, when I looked back
she pressed closer stopped closer
before crossing the gravel path
before leaping through the grass,
her white tail held high.

I watched her become the trees.

Susan B. Auld began writing while growing up on Long Island. A Speech-Language Pathologist and poet, she has been studying and writing modern English-language haiku for the last nine years. Susan, who lives in Buffalo Grove, Illinois, is the author of three books: *Waiting Innocence, Visiting Morning and Other Quiet Places*, and a haiku collection, *Chrysanthemum Dusk*.

A Chocolate Afternoon
by
Mary Jo Balistreri

The Florida sun says *yes* as it sits on my back.
A huge raccoon says *enjoy* as it paws a find from someone's lunch.
The alligator, banked on the berm, doesn't care.

A winding path of rich, dark chocolate courses through my body,
collides with the headache the doctor promised,
chocolate one of his *don'ts*.

I hear the voice I have chosen to ignore, take off my shoes,
walk barefoot in the tide.

Royal terns flock in the February sky. Crowns gleam
as they rise and swoop in auric arabesques.

Pelicans are swans gliding on waves;
ibis, one-legged yogis on sand.

I ask myself, on this opulent afternoon,
is there any other way to live but
exuberantly?

———————

Mary Jo Balistreri is the author of three books of poems and a chapbook.
She has been learning and writing Japanese forms for several years now and
finds haiku, tanka and haibun a wonderful way to be in the moment. Mary
Jo is a member of Grace River Poets, which presents readings for schools,
churches, and women's shelters. Learn more about her
at maryjobalistreripoet.com.

I Am, for the Time, Being
by
Phyllis Beckman

This morning I was musing when
This feeling came along
Reminding me I'm comfy, that
I feel like I belong.

So glad I'm not so worried
About what's next to be
That I miss the present "now"
That life has offered me

When all these special moments
Are noticed one by one
The richness of just living
Can bubble up in fun

So thank you to the giver
Who urges me to take
My time, though it is fleeting,
A mindful life to make!

I am, for the time, being.

———————

Phyllis Beckman lives in Onalaska, Wisconsin, where she writes a poem
every day and shares it with family members and friends. She credits the
Tuesday Edition of the Mississippi Valley Writers Guild of La Crosse,
Wisconsin and the Wisconsin Fellowship of Poets for ongoing inspiration
and encouragement.

What Is Dying?
by
Rev. Luther F. Beecher

I am standing upon the seashore. A ship at my side spreads her white sails
to the morning breeze, and starts for the blue ocean.
She is an object of beauty and strength, and I stand and watch her
until she hangs like a speck of white cloud just where the sea and sky
come down to meet and mingle with each other.
Then someone at my side says, "There! She's gone!"
Gone where? Gone from my sight—that is all.
She is just as large in mast and hull and spar as she was
when she left my side,
and just as able to bear her load of living freight
to the place of her destination.
Her diminished size is in me, and not in her.
And just at that moment when someone at my side says,
"There! She's gone!"
there are other eyes watching for her coming; and other voices
ready to take up the glad shout: "There she comes!"
And that is—"dying."

———————————

Rev. Luther F. Beecher (1813 – 1903) was a Baptist minister and
temperance advocate born in Connecticut. A graduate of Yale, he was a
cousin of Henry Ward Beecher. Rev. Beecher helped establish the Saratoga
Female Seminary at Temple Grove and served as its principal for several
years.

Life Lines
by
Randy Cadenhead

Walk where you have never been
and wonder at the beauty of this world.

Wish for the best, but work,
and for its own reward.

Give more than you receive
and share it freely.

Be moderate in all things,
except goodness.

Wait your turn
and, on occasion, give it away.

Learn, if just to know;
grow wise.

Dream often,
and find a way to live your fondest.

Do all you can
never to hurt another.

Help someone daily;
it will heal your hurt as well.

Read,
for a book can change your life.

Write your own story;
you may change another's world.

Restore something old
and treasure it.

Reward freely,
repay always.

The greatest dignity is in the respect
given to one who is humble.

Obey and serve,
when it is due.

Always do what is right,
but do so ever with kindness.

Be confident in yourself
and humble before all others.

Befriend those who need,
for they can be the truest.

Love wholly and long
one who is worthy.

Give and receive love fully,
for that is the breath of life.

Be kind to all who will accept it,
and be fair to all others.

Beware that some are not good
and avoid, but never fear, them.

Believe in something better,
and live to make it true.

Dig in good earth;
sow new life.

Reap with pride;
cook for pleasure.

Live fully each moment,
for time will not return the chance.

Laugh out loud;
listen always.

Know the taste of longing
and the joy of play.

Listen to the music
you can find in silence.

Sing for the joy of it,
dance to its freedom.

Pray, even when it is hard to believe,
for we were not meant to be alone.

Save for tomorrow,
each day.

Share from your heart
and with your hands.

Forgive as you can,
for we are all only human.

Accept what you cannot change;
remember warmly and wisely.

Stand for something that matters;
treasure memories most of all.

Trust when you can,
but doubt when you ought.

Know that despite it all,
life is good.

———————

Randy Cadenhead is the author of five books, the most recent being *How Not to Write a Poem*. Although he teaches at Emory Law School, you are more likely to find him sailing somewhere in search of the perfect sunset. Randy lives in Decatur, Georgia; learn more about him at www.randycadenhead.com.

In Praise of Doorsteps
by
Janice Canerdy

I think of sunsets I have seen
throughout my many years
from doorsteps where in quiet thought
I've laughed and wiped my tears.

The doorstep is a thinking spot
a place to share my day
with loved ones God has given me,
an altar where I pray.

For children it's a special seat
for rest when school work ends,
where snacks and many laughs are shared
with kindred-spirit friends.

For youths it is a meeting place
where games and dates are planned.
The simple structure serves us all,
according to demand.

Great praise is due life's doorsteps, both
intangible and seen,
and all the portals fore and aft
for all they truly mean.

————————————

Janice Canerdy is a retired high-school English teacher from Potts Camp,
Mississippi. She has been writing poetry since childhood and has had
poems published in many magazines and anthologies. Her first
book, *Expressions of Faith*, was published in 2016. Janice is very involved in
church life and family life. She retired early to keep her grandchildren, who
fill her life with purpose and joy. They also inspire her to write.

Forty Pounds of Moorparks
by
Grace Hughes Chappell

apricots making perfume inside a crate
arrived from the house on the Smartsville Road

"apricots! already?"
people were apt to swoon,
"ah-h, apricots from a tree!"
— as opposed to ... from where? —
but I knew what they meant:
molten gold in the kettle
cooked down for the gods'
breakfast toast, summers past
all summers to come
stolen
saved
caught on a spoon

––––––––––––

Grace Hughes Chappell has lived nearly all of her adult life in northern
California. After raising their children in San Francisco, she and her
husband moved to Mendocino County along a feeder stream of the Eel
River and, for 25 years, have cultivated a garden and an apple orchard there.
Grace's work has been widely published and she is the author of a
chapbook, *ten mile creek almanac*. When she thinks about it, Grace posts at
gracehugheschappell.blogspot.com.

In the Shade of the Tractor's Wheel
by
Peter Christensen

Each day my mother
delivered to the fields
where my father toiled
a mid-day meal
of hard-boiled eggs
coarse wheat bread
buttered yellow as barley
and slathered in wild raspberry jam

Coffee in mason jars
sweetened with molasses
thick with cow's cream
all wrapped in newspaper
and towels
hot to touch

she popped the seal
from the jar
with the edge of the golden lid
poured it
let the fragrant liquid cool
before he sipped the edge
of the green glass cup

Strained muscles dust sin and sweat
washed away by that sweet drink
followed by a little sleep
in the shade of the tractor's wheel

Peter Christensen is a retired guide and park ranger who lives in a remote village on the North Coast of British Columbia. He is the author of five books.

I Saved a Turtle Yesterday
by
Randell Collier

I saved a turtle yesterday; I found him in the road.
He wasn't fast so he got passed by his friend, Mr. Toad.
By the look upon his face, I knew that he was worried,
But we all know the turtle's pace: he simply won't be hurried.
I'm sure the poor thing's life flashed by as the big truck rumbled past,
So I bent down and picked him up and set him in the grass.
He didn't speak (they can't, you know) as down the path he trod,
But just before I turned to go, I'm sure I saw him nod.
Then he paused and, looking back, he smiled as if to say,
"Thank you for your kindness, friend, and your help along the way."

Then I thought of how it is: things just don't go as planned.
All of us, from time to time, may need a helping hand.
But now I know just what I'll do, because I plainly see
If I will just be there for you, maybe you'll be there for me.
And when we've helped each other, we'll both smile and say,
"Thank you for your kindness, friend, and your help along the way."

As I travel this life's road with its obstacles and hurdles,
There are times it truly seems to be much like that turtle's.
The devil tries to run me down with his anger and his wrath
But the good Lord picks me up and sets me on a better path.
And, some day, when at last I see Him, I will smile and say,
"Thank you for your kindness, Lord, and your help along the way."

———————

Randell Collier is a husband, father, and grandfather who dabbles in poetry and occasional songwriting. He lives in the Towanda, Kansas area.

Where You'll Find Me
by
Gail Braune Comorat

I'm no good at route numbers, never sure of east
or south, but I know this road by seasons, by landmarks
memorized the last time I traveled this way.
If you still want me, just head away from the city,

keep an eye out for meadows of bold blue and yellow —
bachelor buttons, wild mustard. Cross the rusted iron bridge
that will lead you to a crossroad —
turn left and keep going until
you see a stand selling Tender Spring Peas and
an orchard of peach trees beyond their bloom. Take your time

as you roll through the old mill town
where elderly men in suspenders and felt hats
doze on planked benches. Wave as you drive by.
You'll pass beneath a thick canopy of elms, and then

there will be a Mennonite farm (yellow siding and pine-
green shutters) with a misspelled sign that offers
Saw Sharpning. You might see some deer in the field.

After that, it's straight on until the road dead-ends
to a graveled lane. Drive as far as it takes you,
park right beside the house.
I'll be on the crooked swing,
rocketing skyward and back, skyward and back,
my eyes on the cove, watching
bald eagles query the river.
I'll be waiting for you.

Gail Braune Comorat is a founding member of Rehoboth Beach Writers
Guild, author of *Phases of the Moon*, and a collaborating poet for *Walking the
Sunken Boards*. She serves as an editor for *Quartet*, an online poetry journal
for women 50 and over, and is a long-time member of several writing
groups in Lewes, Delaware. Gail's work has appeared in *Gargoyle, Grist,
Mudfish, Philadelphia Stories, and The Widows' Handbook*.

The Great Escape
by
Lois Corcoran

When troubles get the best of me
And friends have gone astray,
I have a place I like to go
That isn't far away.

I need no train to take me there,
Nor swift and mighty steed,
For what I do when I am sad
Is find a book to read.

The stories take me everywhere,
I travel in my mind.
Whene'er the hero must move on,
I won't be far behind.

I live his life in all detail.
His thoughts are my thoughts, too.
How can I share a life so rich
And find time to be blue?

So when you're feeling woebegone
And friends are hard to find,
Open up a waiting book
And leave your cares behind.

Lois Corcoran claims she wrote dozens of "awful" poems before turning her pen toward other projects, including a humor column which was carried by a dozen newspapers. She and her husband live in Upstate Michigan, where Lois' current passion is making music.

Road Dog
by
Joe Cottonwood

We're driving fast through farmland
when a roadside man waves his arms:
Slow down! Slow down! A dog, mid-highway.
I stop, blocking the road, turn on flashers.
Rose leaps out. I join her. We're dog people.

Rose can't catch the dog.
The man is shouting "Grab her! Grab her!"
By size and shape the dog is a shepherd,
colored like a beagle, looking friendly as heck
but confused and frantic.

I suspect this shep-beagle just wants
somebody to tell her what to do,
so I crouch and call "Come!"
From the center of the highway she runs
straight to my outstretched hands.
I seize the collar and command "Sit!"
She sits.

The man waddles over and takes her by the collar.
He's overweight, bald with a white beard, bad hips.
He says, "I know where she belongs."

Now I check on the cars behind my flashers,
engines idling. Drivers waiting.
Are they annoyed?
Nope. Big smiles.
Dog people.

Joe Cottonwood is a semi-retired contractor with a lifetime of small jobs
repairing homes. He lives with his high school sweetheart under redwoods
in the Santa Cruz mountains of California, caring for curly-haired dogs and
straight-haired grandchildren. Joe's latest book is *Random Saints*. Learn more
about him at www.joecottonwood.com.

My God
by
Julie Creighton

I don't know why they have to make God so complicated,
all those rules, mysteries, miracles.
They say God talks to prophets
but I'm not impressed.
God talks to me all the time
whispering in my ear.
Sometimes praising, sometime pointing out the error of my ways.
but always at the end of the day,
he comes to bless me
and this is what he has to say.
"You're a slow learner, but it's OK.
Tomorrow, with my help,
Maybe, you'll do better."

———————

Julie Creighton is retired and lives with her husband of 50 years on a ranch in central Texas. Although she has always enjoyed reading, Julie's appreciation for poetry really developed late in life. She began writing poetry after a girls' trip where the theme was to bring and share favorite poems. At the end of the weekend, each wrote an original poem to share with the group. Julie enjoyed this new experience so much that she has begun sharing her experiences and thoughts through poetry.

Ordinary Life
by
Barbara Crooker

This was a day when nothing happened,
the children went off to school
remembering their books, lunches, gloves.
All morning, the baby and I built block stacks
in the squares of light on the floor.
And lunch blended into naptime,
I cleaned out kitchen cupboards,
one of those jobs that never gets done,
then sat in a circle of sunlight and drank ginger tea,
watched the birds at the feeder jostle over lunch's
little scraps. A pheasant strutted from the hedgerow,
preened and flashed his jeweled head.
Now a chicken roasts in the pan, and the children
return, the murmur of their stories dappling the air.
I peel carrots and potatoes without paring my thumb.
We listen together for your wheels on the drive.
Grace before bread. And at the table, actual conversation,
no bickering or pokes. And then, the drift into homework.
The baby goes to his cars, drives them along the sofa's
 ridges and hills. Leaning by the counter, we steal
a long slow kiss, tasting of coffee and cream.
The chicken's diminished to skin & skeleton,
the moon to a comma, a sliver of white,
but this has been a day of grace in the dead of winter,
the hard cold knuckle of the year, a day that unwrapped itself
like an unexpected gift, and the stars turn on,
order themselves into the winter night.

———————

Barbara Crooker's award-winning poems have appeared in numerous
magazines, journals, and anthologies and have been featured on the BBC,
the ABC (Australian Broadcasting Company), and in the Poetry
at Noon series at the Library of Congress. Recipient of many fellowships
and residencies in the U.S., as well as in Ireland and France, she was also a
Grammy finalist for her part in the audio version of the popular
anthology, *Grow Old Along with Me—the Best is Yet to Be*. Barbara lives in
Fogelsville, Pennsylvania; learn more about her
at www.barbaracrooker.com.

Seeking Joy
by
William Henry Davies

Joy, how I sought thee!
Silver I spent and gold,
On the pleasures of this world,
In splendid garments clad;
The wine I drank was sweet,
Rich morsels I did eat—
Oh, but my life was sad!
Joy, how I sought thee!

Joy, I have found thee!
Far from the halls of Mirth,
Back to the soft green earth,
Where people are not many;
I find thee, Joy, in hours
With clouds, and birds, and flowers—
Thou dost not charge one penny.
Joy, I have found thee!

William Henry Davies (1871-1940) was a Welsh poet who started out as a rounder but ended up a respected poet. Raised by grandparents after his father died and his mother remarried, William was inclined toward a life of adventure; he travelled by boat to North America repeatedly before losing a leg in attempting to jump a train. He eventually returned to England, wrote a book about his wandering years, paid and starved his way into becoming a published poet and, eventually, gained equal standing with such contemporaries as Yeats and Ezra Pound.

After Travel
by
Gail Entrekin

When you return from your travels, those
who remember you went ask how it was.
They ask in the most general terms
meaning they would like the most general answer,
pleasant and short. But if you are lucky, two or three
will be curious, or have time, or love you
enough to say, pulling forward a chair,
What were your three favorite things? or
What is the thing you will never forget?
And then you will need to know
how to become a raconteur if you wish to share
anything at all from the great montage:
San Marco Square in moonlight,
bike riding in the freezing air along an Amsterdam
canal, the peasant woman in headscarf outside
your post-Yugoslavian complex in the bleak playground
of Ljubljana, her cloth bags, her large-eyed pale child,
your sense of isolation and the bitter cold. You choose
your favorite days, sweet as apples in a green bowl,
or your terrible days, bitter as icy water rising up
your legs, but either way they're really yours alone,
will go with you, finally,
when you go.

————————

Gail Entrekin lives in the hills of San Francisco's East Bay, where she is a
poet, a quilt designer and maker, a hiker (with her dog, Molly Bloom), an
editor of *Canary Lit Magazine*, a former teacher of creative writing and
English, a singer-around-the-house, a caregiver for her husband (who is
blind and has Parkinson's disease), a grandmother of eight, a small-time
gardener, and co-publisher (with her husband) of a small press called Hip
Pocket Press. Learn more about her at http://gailruddentrekin.com/.

Existence 101
by
Jayne Jaudon Ferrer

Here's what I think:
God put us here to do more than take up space
and mow grass.
We are here to contribute something.
Teachers, doctors, scientists, artists—all shoo-ins.
Pro ballplayers, fashion designers—on shaky ground.
Most of us fall somewhere in between.
Yesterday, for example, I made my family's favorite dessert,
smiled at a solemn old man,
and let three strangers go ahead of me in the turn lane.
Today, however, I fear I owe the universe a sizable debt
for the peace, love, and joy my black mood
sucked straight out of the ozone.
So be it.
We are not perfect, and there is no grade.
There is only opportunity.
Carpe carefully.

———————

Jayne Jaudon Ferrer is the author of four collections of poetry and a
nonfiction book about games. She speaks frequently at churches, schools,
and writing-related events and her work has appeared in hundreds of
publications. Jayne is the founder and editor of YourDailyPoem.com and
enjoys reading, music, old movies, gardening, hiking, and good
conversation. A native Floridian, Jayne has lived in Greenville, South
Carolina, since 1994. Learn more about her at www.jaynejaudonferrer.com.

Beach Reverie
by
Dorothy K. Fletcher

green like jade
warm ocean waters
roll in with wild horse legs

all ajumble
galloping at the ends
of the color

diminishing in size
as they draw near
the end of the world

only to slide back
to be in the race again
I could watch this

joy forever but I
close my eyes
to absorb the sounds

of wild waves
of hungry gulls
of children playing

clean breezes wash
over warmed skin
basking in gold

I let myself melt
into beach colors
beiges and blond

like sands
my jade eyes open
my blue soul rises

running with water
horses to horizons
I can only imagine

this is my heaven

Dorothy K. Fletcher is retired after 35 years of teaching English in Jacksonville, Florida. Her poetry and articles have appeared in nearly a hundred publications, and she is the author of nine books. Dorothy lives with her husband, Hardy, close to their children and grandchildren. A former columnist for *The Florida Times Union*, Dorothy's anecdotes about life in Jacksonville in the '50s, '60s, and '70s earned her a Preservation Award from the Jacksonville Historic Preservation Commission in 2011. Learn more about her at www.rememberingjacksonville.com.

There Will Be Stars
by
Patricia L. Goodman

There will be tears, for we are only human.
There will be toil. A bluebird doesn't get
from field to field by wishing.
There will be peonies, for their beauty fosters
more peonies.
Sometimes there will be cold, to prepare
for summer's peaches.
Sometimes there will be laughter, to lighten
hours of hardship.
There will be love and the warmth
of a child's hand.
There will be lilting music.
And there will be loss and loneliness.
But if, on a clear and moonless night you stand
on a hilltop away from the haze of civilization,
where the dazzle of a billion, trillion heavenly bodies
glitters the sky, settles around your shoulders,
you will know in your heart, that no matter the strife,
there will always be stars.

Patricia L. Goodman is a retired horse breeder and teacher who enjoys
singing, gardening, writing, musical theater, and spending time with her
family. Patricia, who lives in Delaware, is the author of three books—
Unbridled, *Closer to the Ground* and *Walking with Scissors*.

Everyday Things
by
Richard Greene

The sky that's always with us
in light or darkness,
a radiance of moon,
the seasons,
the tree behind the house,
the birds that sing so tirelessly in its branches,
the shadow of leaves on a wall,
a spouse's touch.
Should we cherish them any the less
for being commonplace?

————————

Richard Greene, of Nyack, New York, began writing poetry in the 8th
grade, inspired by the opening lines of Longfellow's "Evangeline," which he
was required to read in class. But poetry fell by the wayside for almost forty
years as a busy career in international development consumed his life. As
retirement approached, however, Richard's interest in poetry returned; he is
now the author of a book, *Explorations*, and shares a weekly poem on his
website, www.greenepage.net.

A Creed
by
Edgar Guest

Let me be a little kinder,
Let me be a little blinder
To the faults of those around me,
Let me praise a little more;
Let me be, when I am weary
Just a little bit more cheery,
Let me serve a little better
Those that I am striving for.

Let me be a little braver
When temptation bids me waver,
Let me strive a little harder
To be all that I should be;
Let me be a little meeker
With the brother that is weaker,
Let me think more of my neighbor
And a little less of me.

Let me be a little sweeter,
Make my life a bit completer
By doing what I should do
Every minute of the day;
Let me toil, without complaining,
Not a humble task disdaining,
Let me face the summons calmly
When death beckons me away.

––––––––––

Edgar Guest (1881 - 1959) was born in England, but moved with his family
to Detroit, Michigan, when he was ten years old. He worked for more than
sixty years at the *Detroit Free Press*, publishing his first poem at the age of
seventeen, then going on to become a reporter and columnist whose work
was featured in hundreds of newspapers around the country. Edgar is said
to have written some 11,000 poems during his lifetime, most of it
sentimental, short, upbeat verse. Critics often derided his work, but
America adored him. He was known as the "People's Poet," served as
Michigan's poet laureate, hosted a long-running radio show and TV show,
and published more than twenty books.

Morning Smile
by
Merle Hazard

Sunshine sparkles
on dewy petals of
the Knockout rose bush.

A furry brown chipmunk
nibbles his breakfast
on the bird feeder.

Everything may not be
all right with the world,
but some things are!

Merle Hazard lives in Macon, Georgia. Her poems have appeared in a number of secular and inspirational publications. A home health and hospice nurse for many years, she worked as a director of programs as well as at bedsides. Now retired, Merle enjoys reading, walking, playing bridge, feeding the birds, her garden, and spending time with friends and family.

Weekend Plans
by
David Holper

In a talk I recently heard, the speaker said
that at 50, a man has less than
1500 weekends left in his life.
Having chewed on this fact for the last week,
I now realize that my 1499th weekend is coming.

And so I'm making big plans:
On this 1499th remaining Saturday,
I plan to grade a stack of student papers.
But knowing that there are only so many of these
Saturdays to sit through,
I am planning on writing the most
remarkable comments and grades
I have ever composed.

Instead of pointing out where the prose clunks,
I will say that the sentence over which I stumble
reminds me of a '62 Fiat convertible
I once owned, a car that ran well enough
when I bought it,
until I rear-ended a truck one day
and the front end crumbled
pushing the radiator back just enough
that the fan chewed a hole through
the back end,
the blades not only making an unearthly racket,
but also bleeding the radiator dry
and leaving a green stain on the pavement.

And instead of pointing out that a comma is not a coma,
that *noone* and *alot* are two words,
that a manor is a large country house,
(in a manner of speaking)
and that collage
is not an institution of higher learning,
I will point out to them that Shakespeare, too,
invented new spellings and words
so that rather than see their grades as a kind
of condemnation,
they might rather embrace these marks as a sort of celebration

of their wild and anarchic spirit
which has emancipated itself from all bounds,
from all pedestrian, prosaic concerns
on this glorious, remaining 1499th Saturday.

———————

David Holper has done a little bit of everything: taxi driver, fisherman, dishwasher, bus driver, soldier, house painter, bike mechanic, bike courier, and teacher. He is the author of two collections of poetry, *64 Questions* and *The Bridge,* and his award-winning poems have appeared in numerous literary journals and anthologies. David teaches English at College of the Redwoods and lives in Eureka, California, far enough from the madness of civilization that he can still see the stars at night and hear the Canada geese calling.

Now
by
Bob Kimberly

Clouds float across the sky,
a gentle breeze moves the leaves,
and the sun shines down
evoking memories of summers past
when days were long and busy
with dogs and horses, barns and tractors.

Life was full, and we were young.
We thought we had it all,
but that's behind us in a different time.
Today our lives are slow and quiet,
and the dearest thing
I have left to share with you is now.

———————

Bob Kimberly grew up in Wisconsin, then spent time in Western North
Carolina and Massachusetts before ending up in the Pacific Northwest.
After retiring and downsizing from a horse farm to a small backyard with
one bird feeder, he joined a creative writing class seventeen years ago to
keep busy. Since then, he has self-published four books of poetry plus
annual chapbooks used as Christmas presents for family and friends.

Together
by
Arlene Gay Levine

We are in this together.
Everything belongs to all of us: rough days
and rainbows, dirty wash and sun-drenched skies,
hungry hearts and fall harvests, angry words
and healing prayers. Whether you put your
foot in the water or not, the waves will roll
in and out. The starling in the snow finds
the squirrel's discarded stash.
Smile. Breathe. Life goes on.
Be grateful.
We are in this together.

Arlene Gay Levine is the author of *39 Ways to Open Your Heart: An Illuminated Meditation* and *Movie Life*. Her poetry and prose have appeared in *The New York Times*, an off-Broadway show, the radio, and more than 30 anthologies and journals. Arlene has served as a judge for Illinois and Virginia state poetry society contests, and she is the creator/facilitator of Logos Therapy™, a transformational writing process. Arlene lives with her husband in New York City, where she tends a garden of words, roses, and herbs. Learn more about her at http://www.arlenegaylevine.com.

Behind the Façade
by
Lori Levy

On the way to the pumpkin patch with the petting farm and
the tractor rides, the bales of hay and the shoe-house,
my grandson announces his decision:
he never wants to be a grown-up
because grown-ups have to work and that's no fun.
He'll be a kid forever.

We hide behind our bodies, bigger, fuller, rougher than his.
He doesn't guess our secret—how we sit
in our offices, at our desks, in our swivel chairs,
squirming to be kids. Tell me it's not true:
your legs itch to climb those monkey bars in the schoolyard,
blood rushing to your head to hang upside
down from a rung at the top.
The urge is there, the child in you begging
for a break from work, restless for release—
for heart-pumping play in the woods or the surf,
in a vacant lot down the street, on a stoop, cement.
A hill is not a mound of grass and earth, but a call to action:
Come, it says, like you did when you were young.
Race down my slope, tripping, tumbling, shrieking your laughter
to the sky as you roll to a stop at the bottom.
You know you want to swing, pumping hard—or, at least,
to be pushed on a swing or carried on a back or on shoulders
that lift you to the ceiling and understand your need
to be tall for a moment and then small again
at nighttime, when you're ready to let go of the day
and be read to and cuddled; to be tucked in,
precious and adored.

If none of this is true, tell me why you're smiling.
Or why you're not—why you're gripping your chair,
hanging on for dear life.

Lori Levy's poems have been published in numerous literary journals and
anthologies in the U.S., the U.K., and Israel. She and her family live in Los
Angeles now, but Lori grew up in Vermont and spent part of her adult life
in Israel. She enjoys reading, writing, and spending time with family and
friends, especially in nature. Her grandchildren keep her entertained, on her
toes and, occasionally, inspire poems.

My Quiet Place
by
Bobbi Martino

There's a place in the woods that only I know—
A place in the wood where I can go
When I'm tired or worried or down in the dumps
When I feel that I'm getting most all of the bumps.
It's so quiet that when I am there, I forget
All my troubles and worries and cares, and I let
The whole world go right by me and not even see
That I'm hiding there from it and trying to be
As quiet, as quiet as ever I can
So I won't break the quiet unbroken by man.
His planes and his trains and his cars and fast pace
Have never been heard of, in my quiet place.

———————

Bobbi Martino grew up in rural Maine, with plenty of woods to wander. Daughter and granddaughter of gifted gardeners, she is a lifelong lover of nature in general and trees, flowers, and the ocean, in particular. A retired nurse and mother of three, Bobbi spends her time these days in or near the ocean—as often as is possible—in Plymouth, Massachusetts. She enjoys sewing, flowerpot gardening, reading, and writing rhymes for her five grandchildren.

Sunrise
by
Timothy McQuade

A small line of lightening sky
Thin bright blue
Then purple into orange as it widens and rises
Brightening with promise
I see it, I feel it
Promise, Grace, Hope
This new day of life
I relish it, I drink it in
This sunrise
I see others oblivious, imprisoned in cars
In routines, in impatience with traffic
In plans for the day
Seeing their day
And seeing nothing at all
Missing the sunrise
Missing life
This small line of brightening light stands and calls them
It calls me
I pray I will not ever be so imprisoned again
As to fall back into sleep and to miss it
This sunrise
This small line of brightening light
How beautiful, How wonderful
I give thanks

––––––––––

Timothy McQuade enjoys the practice of writing poetry. Over the years, he had written poems occasionally, but now it has become a larger part of his life. Timothy says writing poetry encourages him to slow down and experience what could easily be missed in a rushed life. When not writing, Timothy works as an interim pastor, serving churches experiencing transition in pastoral leadership.

Give Me Maps
by
Diane Lee Moomey

I'll search for you, MapQuest or Yahoo;
print out the words to send me
spiraling to your front door. Eventually.
Or I'll Google, click "satellite", note
the color of your mailbox; your boat,
how many dandelions in the yard.

Instruct my 'droid
to call out in loud voice,
(male or female, my choice), to
"turn left at next intersection,
turn left at next intersection,
turn left at next intersection."

I'll do these things with grace, for you,
but oh for pure adventure, do
give me maps, give me paper, give me maps!

Give me ink: new, or with piney residue
of picnic tables past. I'll unfold
their vast beauty, fill the dashboard,
fold, refold, behold the North
and South of them, the scale of miles;
drop mustard onto Wichita, count inches
to Vancouver, Cheboygan, Dubuque.

Give me maps! Maps, and children who'll demand
while dripping jam on Alabama, who'll demand—
of course they will demand— to know
if we are There yet.

Diane Lee Moomey is a painter and poet living in Half Moon Bay,
California, where she is co-host of the monthly reading series, Coastside
Poetry. Her award-winning work has been published in numerous journals
and her fifth poetry collection, *Make for Higher Ground,* will be released in
2021. Besides writing poetry, Diane enjoys long walks beside the ocean,
reading mysteries, and painting in watercolors. Learn more about her
at https://www.pw.org/content/diane_moomey and
www.dianeleemoomeyart.com.

A Drawer Filled to Overflowing
by
Wendy Morton

It's the sails of spatulas I praise,
their sturdy masts
ready for any wind
and the Vollrath ice cream scoop,
that clicks with perfect gears
beside the three clanking whisks
in the French style:
elegant stirrers of sauces,
of olive oil, balsamic vinegar;
beaters of eggs, next to
their coy stepsister,
the coiled whisk. I praise

the sensible wooden spoons
with their burns, stains and cracks;
their comfortable fit in any hand,
and Grandmother's ladle:
Rogers' triple plate, worn thin,
pitted by too many soups,
and the rolling pin still
smelling of butter and blueberries.

We need more in the world
that clanks, whirls and scoops.
We need the familiar,
the worn, the cracked.

We need lovely disorder;
predictable, exuberant clutter
overflowing into our hands.

Wendy Morton, a retired insurance investigator, is the author of six books
of poetry, a memoir—*Six Impossible Things Before Breakfast*—in which her
adventures as a corporate sponsored poet are revealed, and a set of poetry
postcards. Founder of Canada's Random Acts of Poetry project, she
received a Meritorious Service Medal for her work with The Elder Project.
Wendy lives in Sooke, British Columbia.

Life Lessons from My Dog
by
Maryalicia Post

Greet each morning like a welcome surprise,
each family member as if they lit up my world
Delight in what I have to eat, in the freedom to walk
and if confined to old paths
sniff out something interesting each day
If it's bright, relax in a patch of sunlight
If it's dark, curl up in my favorite chair
Yawn and stretch when it suits me
Bark only when necessary
Be happy for a pat on the back and a soft word
Don't think about yesterday
or tomorrow
Give love and watch it come back

Maryalicia Post grew up in New York City, but has lived most of her life in
Dublin, Ireland. She is now retired after a 70-year journalism career that
included stints as a travel writer, advertising copywriter, medical editor,
book author, and poet. When she wasn't writing, Maryalicia often made
time for cross-country horseback riding. Read about some of her favorite
destinations—literally from the Arctic Circle to Zanzibar—at
https://maryaliciapost.com/.

The Feeling of Earth on My Fingers
by
Barbara Quick

Sometimes I like to take the gloves off—
to pull the weeds and gather the harvest
bare-handed. To remember this is earth,
not dirt. To keep my body's memory
fresh—here where the roots twine down,
searching for sustenance. Here
where the worms create their magic:
this will be my bed. A flowerbed,
perhaps. A vegetable garden
blushing with its own abundance.

These plants, all of them, are wiser
than I will ever be. They know
how to drink the mist and make the most
of every photon of sunlight
and moonlight, too, living ever
in their moment of life.

Praise the wisdom of the wanderers
who kiss the earth upon at last
returning home.

Barbara Quick is an award-winning novelist and poet based in Sonoma
County, California. Her debut poetry chapbook, *The Light on Sifnos*—from
which this poem comes—was awarded the 2020 Blue Light Press Poetry
Prize. Barbara's 2007 novel, *Vivaldi's Virgins*, translated into 12 languages, is
currently in development as a mini-series. An avid dancer, hiker, and nature
lover, Barbara divides her time between writing and tending to her edible
gardens. Learn more about her at www.barbaraquick.com.

Everything About Egypt
by
Edwin Romond

Music was only supposed to last
from 12:20 to one but
on St. Patrick's Day Sister Judith
seemed radiant as star dust
so on we sang
holding the geography of Egypt
for another day. I remember
our forty-two faces lighting
with Sister's love for the songs
of Ireland that afternoon. Egyptian
rivers had to wait while Vito
Carluzzi crooned, "When Irish
Eyes Are Smiling" and Stash
Jankowski belted "Me Father's
Shillelagh." We just kept singing
and singing with the pyramids and
sphinxes growing one day older
for soon it was 1:30, then it was two
in a room filled with fifth graders
and a nun we loved, one
voice beautiful as prayer. And I,
like a lucky leprechaun, found
a pot of gold in the second row
where pretty Jane Ellen Hughes
sang "O Danny Boy" and I dreamed
in green she was really singing
"O Eddie Boy" as we walked hand
in hand along a Galway shore.
So, Sister Judith, lovely lady of God,
know that this boy in the back
remembers when we kept text books
closed to spend all afternoon in song
and that joy is an emerald river
flowing through my soul and all these years
later I need to thank you for everything
about Egypt we did not learn the day
you let the lesson plan go, one March 17th
when none of us could stop the music.

———————

Edwin Romond is a poet, playwright, composer, and educator. Now retired, he taught English for more than 30 years in Wisconsin and New Jersey. Edwin's award-winning work has appeared in numerous literary journals, college textbooks and anthologies, and has been featured on National Public Radio. A native of Woodbridge, New Jersey, Edwin now lives in Wind Gap, Pennsylvania, with his wife and son. Learn more about him at www.edwinromond.com.

Bs Are a Few of My Favorite Things
by
Laura Purdie Salas

Musical beagle with low plaintive baying
Birch trees in mighty winds bending and swaying
Slow bagpipes haunting, while wild church bells ring,
Bs are a few of my favorite things

Butter that's melted on bread—steaming, wispy
Bacon cooked salty and almost-burned crispy
Brownies, bananas, and baked bagel rings
Bs are a few of my favorite things

When the car breaks, when the bills come
When I'm feeling sad
I simply remember my favorite things
And then I don't feel so bad

Sunsets on beaches with boats in the distance
Bathing suit fitting with little resistance
Bonnet shells, sand dollars, pale angel wings
Bs are a few of my favorite things

All of my best friends are struggling writers
Books and now blogs are my daily delighters
Beautiful words always make my brain sing
These are a few of my favorite things

When the book fails, there are no sales
When reviews are bad
I simply remember my favorite things
And then I don't feel so sad

———————

Laura Purdie Salas is the author of more than 130 books for children and teens, including *Bookspeak! Poems About Books*, *Lion of the Sky*, and the *A Leaf Can Be…* series. A former teacher, she believes reading picture books and poems can have a huge impact on a child's life and she loves to inspire and share practical tips through author visits, conferences, and community events. Learn more about Laura at laurasalas.com.

Whispers from a Bench Along the Trail
by
Sara Sarna

Sit here.
I will bear you
and whatever burdens
you carry
while you breathe
the sacred air
of my forest.

Rest here.
I am old and worn
but I will hold
your memories
and dreams
in this place
trouble does not abide.

Tarry here.
There is no need
to hurry.
I was here
before today
and will remain
when you have gone.

Heal here.
And when you are ready
gather up
what is important.
Leave the rest
for the breeze to scatter,
the rain to wash away.

———————

Sara Sarna grew up in a military family and says she was in her early thirties
"before feeling I had roots." She has now lived in Wisconsin for more than
a quarter of a century. Sara has pursued various careers in the course of her
life, including being a teacher, a bank manager, and a healthcare employee,
but her favorite endeavors— "by far," she admits—have been actor and
poet. Sara, whose work has appeared in print, online, and onstage, is the
author of one chapbook, *Whispers from a Bench*, inspired by this poem.

Miracles on a String
by
Larry Schug

This morning one miracle
follows another
like seed beads on a necklace.

The full moon in its descent
illuminates wind-rippled water—
a dance of light.

Snow geese in flight,
fat bodies pink with sunrise,
fly overhead.

Five robins in a crab apple tree
red breasts afire with dawn
nibble on ripe jewels of fruit.

All my senses,
filling like buckets in rain
swell my heart.

Larry Schug is retired after a life of various kinds of physical labor and
currently occupies his time by volunteering as a writing tutor at the College
of St. Benedict/St. John's University writing centers and as a naturalist at
Outdoor U. He's also learning to play a cigar box guitar and is branching
into putting music to words. Larry has published eight books of poems and
lives with his wife, dog, and two cats near a large tamarack bog in St.
Wendel Township, Minnesota.

My Rocking Chair
by
Robert Service

When I am old and worse for wear
I want to buy a rocking-chair,
And set it on a porch where shine
The stars of morning-glory vine;
With just beyond, a gleam of grass,
A shady street where people pass;
And some who come with time to spare,
To yarn beside my rocking-chair.

Then I will light my corn-cob pipe
And dose and dream and rarely gripe.
My morning paper on my knee
I won't allow to worry me.
For if I know the latest news
Is bad,—to read it I'll refuse,
Since I have always tried to see
The side of life that clicks with glee.

And looking back with days nigh done,
I feel I've had a heap of fun.
Of course I guess that more or less
It's you yourself make happiness
And if your needs are small and few,
Like me you may be happy too:
And end up with a hope, a prayer,
A chuckle in a rocking-chair.

Robert Service (1874 - 1958) was a Scottish poet who moved to Canada at
the age of 21. Though he longed to be a trail-blazing cowboy, Robert was,
in fact, a bank clerk. He wandered North America for several years,
working at odd jobs and various bank branches, before finally settling
down in the Yukon Territory. Fascinated by the surroundings and legends
associated with that part of the world, he began writing poems that turned
into *The Spell of the Yukon and Other Verses*. Upon publication in 1907, it was
an immediate success, made Robert wealthy beyond his greatest
expectations, and earned him the nickname "The Bard of the Yukon." The
cabin in the Klondike where he made his home is now a Canadian national
park site.

Snowy Owl Snarls Traffic in Saskatoon
by
Glen Sorestad

Where did you come from, my splendid winged one?
Just passing through en route to harry fields teeming
with mice and voles, your nocturnal vittles?

What a strange perch you chose, this asphalt patch
of road to alight, the mayhem of motorists, here,
in the driveway entrance to a shopping mall.

Look around, snowy star! You've managed to do
what even traffic lights rarely can with certainty —
backed traffic to a standstill with your presence.

Rare sight that you are on any road at any time,
your sudden presence has changed the tenor
of the day, slowed the rush, brought the police

to direct traffic and ensure your safety, summoned
wildlife people to attend to your needs. A tiny moment,
a respite from the usual urban ennui, a news item,

a driver's anecdote, a curiosity, quickly forgotten.
Still, perhaps there's a smidgeon of comfort we
can glean from your visit, that despite our failures

and seeming lack of will to do what's right,
this day suggests that hope manifests itself in
most unexpected places and wondrous ways.

Glen Sorestad is a poet, fiction writer, editor, publisher, anthologist, and public speaker. Author of more than 20 books of poetry and numerous short stories, his work has appeared in more than 75 anthologies and textbooks. Most recently, Glen's book, *Selected Poems from Dancing Birches*, was published in Italy in a bilingual edition. Glen served from 2000-2004 as Saskatchewan's first Poet Laureate and has given public readings of his poetry in every province of Canada, as well as in the U.S. and many parts of Europe. He lives in Saskatoon with his wife, Sonia, who he claims is his "first and most enthusiastic reader and editor." Learn more about Glen at http://canpoetry.library.utoronto.ca/sorestad/index.htm.

Success
by
Bessie Stanley

He has achieved success
who has lived well,
laughed often, and loved much;

who has enjoyed the trust of
pure women,

the respect of intelligent men and
the love of little children;

who has filled his niche and accomplished his task;

who has left the world better than he found it
whether by an improved poppy,
a perfect poem or a rescued soul;

who has never lacked appreciation of Earth's beauty
or failed to express it;

who has always looked for the best in others and
given them the best he had;

whose life was an inspiration;
whose memory a benediction.

———————

Bessie Anderson Stanley (1879 - 1952), a resident of Kansas, wrote this for a magazine contest that asked, "What constitutes success?" Her entry won first place. Bessie's words are often erroneously attributed to Ralph Waldo Emerson and Robert Louis Stevenson, and are often paraphrased, but this is the original version of her poem.

Begin with the Faucet
by
Christine Swanberg

On days when you think there is nothing
to be thankful for,
begin with the faucet you tweak
to the perfect temperature,
the shower cascading,
massaging your neck and spine.
Consider the soft water you rely on
that allows lather to rise on your head,
or the stout hands of the invisible dishwasher
that scrubbed your pots while you slept.
Notice curtains that frame the window
to whatever day will be discovered,
aroma of good coffee brewing
in the timed coffee maker,
about to rev up your engine,
dollop of cream from Oreo cows munching grass,
the toaster, the toast, and marmalade,
grain, crunch, and fruit.
Reach for bifocals on the end table.
Pet the dog or cat who says good morning
with its nose or tail or nudge.
If there is someone to kiss,
know you are blessed.
Open the front door as you do each day
for the paper delivered by the paper boy
on his pre-dawn rounds.
Listen to a sparrow,
then the radio humming and talking,
song or voice that buoys you
in just the first hour of this day.

———————

Christine Swanberg, retired after 35 years of teaching high school, college, and graduate school, is the author of ten books. More than 600 of her award-winning poems have been published in various journals and anthologies. Christine is the recipient of a Mayor's Award for Community Impact, a YWCA Award for the Arts, a Womanspirit Award, and she was recently named as the first official poet laureate in her hometown of Rockford, Illinois.

On the Trail
by
Mark Thalman

At any one point, I can only see so far ahead
or behind. Whenever I get there is when I arrive.

Tell time from the way fir shadows fall.
Call down canyons . . .

Sing with my echo,
a ball that always bounces back.

When my retriever tires of being the leader,
his wet nose behind my knee nudges me forward.

Camping by a small nameless lake,
gather pine cones and pitch to kindle a fire.

Meteors shoot like sparks across constellations,
smolt darting in a stream.

Keep clear of bears. Recite "The Road Not Taken",
so they know I am there.

Chipmunks make the best friends.
If coyotes howl at the moon, join the choir.

Pace myself. Move at a steady beat.
Be persistent as rain.

Mark Thalman, editor of _poetry.us.com_ and author of three books, has been
widely published for four decades. Retired after teaching English in public
schools for 35 years, he is also an artist who enjoys painting wildlife and
seascapes with acrylics. Mark lives in Forest Grove, Oregon; learn more
about him at www.markthalman.com.

Occasionally
by
David M. Tookey

My bike commute—
Descents and climbs
Like most days

And
Occasionally
Something else

A sharp awareness
Light, wind, clouds, rain
Blackberry, tall grass
Wild anise, a sparrow

Movement blends
External and Internal
A gentle
Drift

Friend, if I could tell it
In a word
It would be
Peace

I wish the same for you

David M. Tookey, a retired elementary school teacher, lives in Seattle, Washington. A bicycle is his main mode of transport around town; David says he finds he can tinker with poems in his head as he rides. He also enjoys creating and sharing organic baked goods and taking long walks with family.

Mindfulness
by
Wang Wei

The spring flowers, the autumn moon;
Summer breezes, winter snow.
If useless things do not clutter your mind,
You have the best days of your life.

Wang Wei (698–759) was a Chinese poet, musician, and painter. Both his paintings and his poems focused largely on nature; Wei is considered the founder of Southern Chinese landscape art. Sadly, none of his original paintings are known to have survived, but more than 400 of his poems are preserved in anthologies and collections.

Don't Quit
by
John Greenleaf Whittier

When things go wrong as they sometimes will,
When the road you're trudging seems all up hill,
When the funds are low and the debts are high
And you want to smile, but you have to sigh,
When care is pressing you down a bit,
Rest if you must, but don't you quit.
Life is strange with its twists and turns
As every one of us sometimes learns
And many a failure comes about
When he might have won had he stuck it out;
Don't give up though the pace seems slow—
You may succeed with another blow.
Success is failure turned inside out—
The silver tint of the clouds of doubt,
And you never can tell just how close you are,
It may be near when it seems so far;
So stick to the fight when you're hardest hit—
It's when things seem worst that you must not quit.

John Greenleaf Whittier (1807 - 1892) was one of the "Fireside Poets," called such because their work was popular enough to be read (ostensibly by the fire) in homes all over America. And Whittier was one of those rare poets who actually made a rather comfortable living from the proceeds of his work. Born into a Massachusetts farm family, Whittier was introduced to poetry by one of his schoolteachers. An avid reader and writer early on, Whittier spent much of his working life as an editor, though he had political aspirations as well. He was a staunch abolitionist, and produced two collections of anti-slavery poems, along with an anti-slavery pamphlet that managed to incur the wrath of *both* sides and, effectively, any hopes Whittier had of a political career. Critical opinion on the value of Whittier's poetry is mixed. Some dismiss it as overly emotional, while others believe the heartfelt simplicity is precisely its appeal.

A Morning Prayer
by
Ella Wheeler Wilcox

Let me to-day do something that shall take
 A little sadness from the world's vast store,
And may I be so favoured as to make
 Of joy's too scanty sum a little more.

Let me not hurt, by any selfish deed
 Or thoughtless word, the heart of foe or friend;
Nor would I pass, unseeing, worthy need,
 Or sin by silence when I should defend.

However meagre be my worldly wealth,
 Let me give something that shall aid my kind—
A word of courage, or a thought of health,
 Dropped as I pass for troubled hearts to find.

Let me to-night look back across the span
 'Twixt dawn and dark, and to my conscience say—
Because of some good act to beast or man—
 "The world is better that I lived today."

———————

Ella Wheeler Wilcox (1850-1919) was a popular and prolific poet. Published
and lauded before she even graduated from high school, Ella preferred to
write happy, upbeat poetry and was much beloved for it. The familiar
saying, "Laugh and the world laughs with you, weep, and you weep
alone. . ." comes from her best-known poem, "Solitude." A morally strong
and spiritual person, Ella believed that her purpose on earth was to practice
kindness and service

Cautionary
by
Dana Wildsmith

Mama called to ask if smoke alarms give death cries.
Hers just now squealed, she said,
and then fell to the floor.
Yes, as I've been trying to warn her,
there can be a high rate of failure-to-thrive
among smoke alarms, chairs, pencils,
and such household plunder, which is,
after all, an assemblage of orphans.
Attention is the key to prevention:
rotate your dishes
that the back bowls not feel neglected.
Turn ceiling fans off; allow them to steady themselves.
When a pen dries up, don't let
the other pens watch you throw it away.
Smooth your sheets; unbend page corners;
straighten charleyhorsed rug fringe.
Thank your mailbox for its daily gifts.
At night when you lock your doors,
say a small benediction of tumbler and wood.
Impress your pillow
with useful dreams.

Dana Wildsmith is the author of six collections of poetry and a memoir. Her love of family, nature, music, tradition, and life's simple joys is the focal point of her widely published work, some of which was featured in the highly acclaimed *Listen Here: Women Writing in Appalachia*. A Georgia Author of the Year finalist, Dana was born and raised in rural South Georgia, then traveled extensively as a Navy wife before settling on her family's century-old farm outside Atlanta. Dana enjoys sharing her passion for language by teaching ESL classes and has served as an Artist-in-Residence in the Grand Canyon and Everglades National Park. Learn more about her at www.danawildsmith.com.

Quotidian Marvels
by
Marilyn Zelke Windau

Silver flashes of sunlit birch leaves
A copper penny in the parking lot
The hoot of an owl at midnight
An email from a forgotten friend

Snowflakes on my tongue
An ecstatic monarch hovering milkweed
Music that snares, then dances my feet
The snort of a four-year-old's laughter

An unexpected thank you
Lakeshore wave foam greeting toes
Golden Book's Mr. Dog in sky clouds
Dust glitter in lamplight

Five piglets cuddling

Sautéed onions and garlic in red Bolognese
Bamboo sheets
The fountain of a grey whale's exhale
My portrait in a polished tabletop

Page warmth from the reading lamp
Salt water taffy-filled teeth topography
Whir-breezes through five-needled white pines
Dark roast Kona grinding

Applause from a sea lion

Marilyn Zelke Windau started writing poems at age thirteen, sitting in a
quiet bathtub with a pillow, pen, and notepad. A retired elementary school
art teacher, she finds visual observation to be of great value to the word arts
and her poems tell stories of caught moments in nature and people's lives.
Author of four books of poetry, Marilyn lives with her husband in
Sheboygan Falls, Wisconsin.

Poems to Make You Smile

Chef's Dilemma
by
Rhona Aitken

Calamari, mussels, a chowder, jellied eels …
a succulent collection. A dainty little meal.
A tantalizing tingle from a lemon-flavoured fish,
with a rich and rare aroma from a dark and daring dish.
Tables set and fires lit, silver-ware clean and shining,
waitresses, with pencils poised, awaiting all those dining.
"Your orders, Sir, what is your wish?
"what dishes, if you please?"
"Two steaks, well done—with chips galore,
and lots of frozen peas!"

Rhona Aitken (1925 - 2018) lived all over the world during the course of her life. Author of *The Memsahib's Cookbook*, which she wrote while living in India, Rhona and her husband, Gordon, owned and operated a hotel and restaurant in the U.K. for many years. Toward the end of her life, Rhona lived in a nursing home in Exmouth, England, where she wrote poetry, painted, shared a poem every morning with her fellow residents, and continued to travel—on her 3-wheeler—as long as she was able.

My Daughter at the Age of Reason
by
David Alpaugh

"Will you please get that cat out of your bed!"
I shout, opening Janet's door to say goodbye—
on my way down the hall, out to the garage,
onto the freeway towards work.

"He's full of fleas!"

She draws Marshmallow closer
strokes his white belly
kisses his ears, eyes, nose and whiskers.

"He's full of love," she smiles.

David Alpaugh has been a featured poet at bookstores, colleges, cafes,
and poetry organizations in the San Francisco Bay Area more than 100
times. His first full collection, *Counterpoint*, won the Nicholas Roerich Poetry
Prize from Story Line Press, and his poetry and essays have appeared
in numerous literary journals. David holds degrees in English from Rutgers
University and the University of California, Berkeley, where he was a
Woodrow Wilson and Ford Foundation Fellow. He was also a finalist for
Poet Laureate of California. Learn more about David
at www.davidalpaugh.com.

Baseball in Connecticut
by
Carol Amato

I knew the feeling as well as any boy
hunched over home plate, a flat rock,
legs apart, left in front, bend the knees,
bat back and hands choked up a lot
(the bat was never kid-sized)
hat low squinting against the glare
silent six-word metronome ticking
keep your eye on the ball
keep your eye on the ball.

Bases loaded.
Timmy's hard-ball pitch the same as
when he hurled rocks in our rock fight
wars at Red Rock Quarry still aiming
more for the head than over the plate.

For every concussion he ever
gave my little brother
I swung on the first count,
the crack
electric sting in my palms
the whirl of frayed ball
over the splintered benches
and me sliding to home
a girl
gladly eating dirt.

Carol Amato is a language-learning specialist, a natural science educator,
and the author of ten books for children about threatened and endangered
animals (The *Young Readers Series*, published by Barron's Educational Series,
Inc., and *Backyard Pets, Nature Activities Close to Home*, published by John
Wiley & Sons). Proud of and grateful for her active imagination, she lives in
Massachusetts.

At the Oriental Theater in Milwaukee
by
Stephen Anderson

Something tells me that the little man
in striped short sleeves and a Sears' tie
could really cut loose with a wild, wailing
boogie-woogie on that awesome Kimball concert organ
on stage down at the Oriental Theater,
instead of the take-me-out-to-the-ballgame/true-blue
schmaltz he is probably told to play before the previews
come on. Not that there's anything patently wrong
with his standard repertoire, but that magnificent organ
has got to be capable of so much more, as I'm sure the man is.

Watching him play, I can imagine him suddenly exploding
into a Ray Charles or, heck, even a Jerry Lee Lewis rocking rendition
in which he shakes the sleepy, popcorn-eating, soda swilling place
up a bit, maybe even bringing those exotic moldings and fixtures to life
before the main feature sparkles from the screen.

And so, every time I'm sitting there waiting for the big screen fare,
I'll imagine how nice it would be if he could, just once,
snap out of the corral he's in, out of all that has been constrained inside,
and make hulk-like all that stuff barely breathing there.

Stephen Anderson is an award-winning poet and translator from
Milwaukee, Wisconsin whose work has appeared in numerous print and
online journals and has been featured on the Milwaukee NPR-affiliate
WUWM Lake Effect Program. Six of his poems formed the text for a
chamber music composition, *The Privileged Secrets of the Arch* that was
performed by two members of the Milwaukee Symphony Orchestra and an
opera singer. Stephen is the author of three chapbooks and two full length
books; a new collection, *High Wire*, is forthcoming.

Flight 404. LA—New York City
by
Diana Anhalt

As the plane barrels down the runway and lifts off, delirious with speed,
someone kicks against my seatback. Then I hear him. A five-year old?
Awesome, dad! Where are we now? We're still in California, says his father.
How can you tell if the clouds get in the way? What's a cloud?

A cloud's made up of droplets of water, so tiny you never see them,
so light they float and—Can I have another cookie please? And now?
Where are we now? he asks through Arizona, Colorado, Illinois…
And what keeps our plane from falling from the sky?

See those engines? They push back the air that moves the plane
forward. Look at the shape of that wing. More air passes under
than over and that causes …The boy cries: *That's the stupidest thing*
I've ever heard. You've made it all up.

The father clears his throat. *How about this? Angels live in those clouds.*
They carry the plane. On their backs. Silence. Then I hear the child.
Yes, that's what happens, I think.

––––––––––

A former resident of Mexico City, Diana Anhalt now lives in Atlanta,
Georgia. A former high school teacher, editor, and civic leader, she is the
author of *A Gathering of Fugitives: American Political Expatriates in Mexico 1947-
1965, Walking Backward,* five chapbooks, and numerous essays, short stories,
and book reviews in both English and Spanish.

To Do List
by
Rob Baker

Atop ragged-edged scratch paper
I write "Mon." and under this
copy Sun.'s uncrossed-off items:
"buy birdseed," "b-day e-card to Adele,"
"call re: basement leak," "bring ashes to cemetery."

I notice one task on the Sunday list
("Pour boiling H2O down drains")
that I did but forgot to cross off,
so I scratch it out now.
Then I remember: this morning
I polished my black shoes—
though this wasn't on the list—
so I write "polish shoes"
then draw a line through it.

Creating and destroying lists
brings a certain sense of satisfaction,
and of futility.
My friend, a psychologist,
(who witnessed my list-making habits on overdrive
when she visited during my eight-day hospice vigil)
said, "List-making gives the illusion of control."

Onto the Mon. list I copy "Start exercising,"
an item that first appeared in May, 2002,
and ever since has been transferred daily.
I've never had the pleasure of scratching it off,
but its presence on repeated lists underscores
the sincerity of my determination to do it
soon.

Rob Baker teaches English at Barrington High School in Barrington,
Illinois. Author of numerous short stories and freelance articles, he credits
the Palatine, Illinois, library's "Second Saturday Poetry Workshop," for
constant inspiration and encouragement.

King Spud
by
Nick Balmforth

I have doubts on sprouts but peas, they please,
And parsnips give me pleasure,
But of all the veg, I give this pledge:
Potatoes are my treasure.
Chipped or baked or mashed or boiled,
Tossed in a pan when gently oiled,
The common spud is really great—
A must on every dinner plate.

Cometh the meal, cometh the hour,
Some folk favor the cauliflower.
Parsnip, turnip, marrow, swede . . .
All have their place when we need to feed.
But whilst all have their turn, and some need to wait,
The veggie that's certain on every plate—
Watering the mouth, exciting taste buds—
The humble, the versatile, ubiquitous spuds.

They may not be pretty, they may have no sheen,
No carroty orange, no broccoli green,
No cabbage-y colors of reds, greens or whites,
No beet-rooty purple—all fanciful sights.
But for full satisfaction, for all-round delight,
For full English breakfasts or suppers at night,
For buffets or banquets, fast food or set lunch,
The potato is king: the best of the bunch!

———————

Nick Balmforth is a retired safety inspector of children's indoor play centers. His primary published work has been in the field of safety standardization for the British and European indoor play industry and he was awarded an MBE (Member of the Most Excellent Order of the British Empire) for his work in 2012. Nick is also a successful voice-over artist and, in addition to poetry, enjoys jazz. He lives in Staffordshire, England.

Horseplay
by
George Bilgere

I am floating in the public pool, an older guy
who has achieved much, including tenure,
a child, and health insurance including dental.

I have a Premier Rewards Gold Card
from American Express, and my car
is large. I have traveled to Iceland.
In addition, I once met Toni Morrison
at a book signing and made some remarks
she found "extremely interesting." And last month
I was the subject of a local news story
called "Recyclers: Neighbors Who Care." In short,
I am not someone you would take lightly.

But when I begin to playfully splash my wife,
the teenaged lifeguard raises her megaphone
and calls down from her throne, "No horseplay in the pool,"
and suddenly I am twelve again, a pale worm
at the feet of a blond and suntanned goddess,
and I just wish my mom would come pick me up.

———————

George Bilgere has lived in Japan and Spain but currently lives in Cleveland, Ohio. A teacher at John Carroll University, he is the author of six collections of poetry. George and his family often spend summers in Germany, where they spend the days bicycling, exploring the city, and goofing off. Learn more about George at http://www.georgebilgere.com.

From My Mother's Kitchen: An Alphabet Poem
by
Pat Brisson

Food my mother made for us
Food from A to Zed;

Apple pie with a flaky crust made from Crisco,
Beef stew (with too much gristle),
Chocolate chip cookies from the Tollhouse recipe,
Dates stuffed with walnuts and coated with sugar,
Eggnog at Christmas time,
French toast with butter and cinnamon sugar,
Ginger ale (stirred until flat) for upset stomachs,
Hamburgers and hot dogs on the 4th of July,
Ice cream — Breyer's coffee for her and Neapolitan for us,
Junket rennet custard, a slippery, slidey treat,
Ketchup on our meatloaf,
Ladyfingers with fresh strawberries and whipped cream,
Mincemeat pies at the holidays, (eaten only by the grown-ups),
Noodles, broad and buttery,
Oatmeal cookies flavored with lemon,
Potatoes, usually boiled,
Quick bread, mostly date and nut,
Ravioli from Chef Boyardee,
Spaghetti with meat sauce,
Tapioca pudding with cinnamon on top,
Upside down peach cake,
Vanilla pudding served on steamed apples and yellow cake,
Watermelon slices with too many seeds,
10X confectioners sugar dusted on top of lemon pound cake,
Yeast bread warm from the oven with butter melting into it,
Zwieback when we were very young.

Food she baked and cooked and boiled
To keep her family fed.

––––––––––

Pat Brisson is a former elementary school teacher and librarian. She has been writing picture books and easy-to-read chapter books for nearly 30 years. Pat coordinates Project Storybook, a program at Edna Mahan Correctional Facility for Women in Clinton, New Jersey, which allows incarcerated mothers to select, record and mail books and tapes to their children. She received the N. J. Governor's Volunteer Award in Human

Services for this wonderful project. Pat lives in Phillipsburg, New Jersey; learn more about her at www.patbrisson.com.

LuRay Love
by
Jan Chronister

They sit behind cupboard doors
   invisible
pastel shades of pink, blue, yellow, green
   glowing in the dark.

They were my mother's wedding china
   each piece stamped with
its manufacture date: 1939, 1942,
   every holiday meal reflected on those blushing plates.

In '46 my sister was born
   blonde curls, bright eyes
hands getting what they wanted.

I arrived three years later
   middle child, second girl
followed by the blessed boy.

Always the black sheep
   misbehaving
   sneaking cigarettes
   climbing out windows
   far-removed
   never filling parents' wishes.

But I am the one with the dishes.

Jan Chronister, a retired teacher of English and Creative Writing, lives in the woods near Maple, Wisconsin. The author of three chapbooks and two full-length poetry collections, she is serving as president of the Wisconsin Fellowship of Poets from 2015-2021. Learn more about Jan at www.janchronisterpoetry.wordpress.com.

Dog in Charge
by
Ginny Lowe Connors

That thing they call a vacuum cleaner
needs to be killed, but when it roars and screams
they feel sorry for it, push it out of my way
and drag me from it just as I'm about
to save them from it. They hide the beast
in a closet when it finally quiets down.
Hideous creature! I know it's there.

The doorbell is strangers trying to get in.
If my people greet them as friends, I allow
entrance. Must jump on them to sniff
out intentions. My people so clueless,
they'd let anyone in—murderers, salesmen,
the no-good neighbors who live with a cat.

My man goes away for hours.
I patrol, nap with one eye open, perk an ear up
for his car. He returns slump-shouldered
carrying his case, his coffee mug. Smells like paper,
dust, the blah blah blah of too much talk.
So I drag him outside.

His nose is blind; he doesn't get
the messages on bushes, trees, or hydrants.
But the wind and the sky, he gets those.
He throws a ball, calls out like a kid.
See how the corners of his mouth
begin to turn up.

It takes a dog to notice these things.

————————

Ginny Lowe Connors is a retired English teacher in West Hartford,
Connecticut. She has published several collections of poems,
including *Toward the Hanging Tree: Poems of Salem Village*, and she has edited a
number of poetry anthologies, such as *Forgotten Women: A Tribute in Poetry*.
Ginny runs a small press, Grayson Books, and co-edits *Connecticut River
Review*, a national poetry journal. Learn more about her
at <u>www.ginnyloweconnors.com</u>.

Garden Bugs
by
Linda Tillis Crosby

Planning, tilling, planting,
All done with love and care.
Soon those little plants appear
Where once the ground was bare.

I grab my gloves, put on my hat,
And hurry out the door.
Can't wait to see what's up today;
Should I plant some more?

I want some for my neighbors,
for the rabbits and the deer,
For the food bank and the mission,
Who feed the homeless there.

Beans are blooming, corn is tall,
Tomatoes big and red...
But what is that? Bugs everywhere!
I look around with dread.

I pinch and pull those critters
Till night at last draws near,
Then drag myself inside my house
To fix a cup of cheer.

Dozing off, I smugly think,
My garden is pest-free!
I got you, bugs! But, oh! that itch!
Perhaps the bugs got me!

———————

Linda Tillis Crosby is a mother and grandmother from Chapmansboro,
Tennessee. Retired after 41 years in the banking industry, she now spends
her time gardening, walking, enjoying nature, and spending time with her
family. Linda sings in her church choir, works part-time as a school bus aide
for children with special needs, and enjoys writing as a hobby.

Chaperone
by
Kay B. Day

One girl leans back against the wall, top row
on the bleachers. Music ricochets off each still
and moving surface. To speak is to shout. Bare
need bear hugs this girl, bowed head to slumped
shoulders. I regret my age. I long for braces
on my teeth and pimples on my face,
budding hips and breasts. I'd like to take
these bleachers two at a time, play-punch
her arm and relay gossip that the other
kids could overhear. I picture us
laughing at the girls we'd like to know,
but can't. We swing and sway and do
the chicken dance, then concoct a plot to get
my mom to take us out for pizza after. We send
our secrets spinning around this sweaty gym.

———————

Kay B. Day's award-winning fiction, nonfiction, and poetry has appeared regularly in top daily newspapers, magazines, and websites. Her collection, *A Poetry Break*, won the Florida Writer's Association poetry book of the year award, and was chosen as a finalist in the Southeastern Booksellers Association "Best of…" competition. Kay was one of three poets invited to present at the U.S. Library of Congress for "Florida Poets Arrive." A longtime columnist for *The Writer*, one of the nation's oldest magazines for writers, she now writes the "Undercovered" column for Patreon and speaks to various groups about media and writing. A member of The Authors Guild and the American Society of Journalists and Authors, Kay lives in Jacksonville, Florida.

Funeral Arrangements
by
Barbara Eknoian

I want my funeral to be in a bright cheery room
filled with daisies, dahlias, and Queen Anne's lace.
I don't like dark places, but I'd prefer a closed casket.
I never liked people staring at me.
Instead, they could place my photograph on top.
Maybe the black and white snapshot of me posing
in my striped bathing suit when I was sixteen.

I hope my family forgets about the time
I ran around the house screaming that a mouse
was chasing me. It was only a ball of string.
I want my kids to forgive me and never mention
the wild Halloween costumes I concocted.
Suzie looked like Dopey the Dwarf with
over-sized rubber ears and a stocking ski cap;
Bobby was supposed to be The Jolly Green Giant
with Crisco and green food dye smeared on his face.
They looked just fine to me.

For a hymn, I'd choose something livelier than
Rock of Ages, and a little more subdued
than *When the Saints Come Marching In.*
A perfect gravesite would be on the top of a hill
with a maple tree shading my plot. It should be
in an old cemetery where they still allow
tombstones, so my epitaph could read,
I tried, Lord, I tried.

————————

Barbara Eknoian lives in La Mirada, CA with her extended family. She
enjoys writing poetry and novels, and much of her material is triggered
from growing up New Jersey. Barbara's latest novel is *Hearts on Bergenline
Avenue*, and her latest poetry chapbook is *Life is But a Dream.*

The Twelve Months
by
George Ellis

Snowy, Flowy, Blowy,
Showery, Flowery, Bowery,
Hoppy, Croppy, Droppy,
Breezy, Sneezy, Freezy.

George Ellis (1753- 1815) was an English satirist who sometimes wrote under the pseudonym "Sir Gregory Gander." The son of a Jamaican planter, George attended Westminster School and graduated from Trinity College at Cambridge. Besides writing prose and poetry, he also produced a number of political cartoons and spent some time working in diplomatic and embassy affairs. A good friend of Sir Walter Scott, George wrote and published several books and started at least one newspaper.

Toddler
by
Michael Escoubas

He's getting into everything
and just a little in the way.

He can't seem to process
that the cat doesn't like
heavy objects heaved at her.

He can't seem to process
that the dolls on the chair
are 100 years old and not
to be handled by their hair.

He can't seem to process
that my teeth won't lift
out of my mouth tug as he might.

He can't seem to process
that the computer keys
don't like his plastic hammer.

What then can he process?
That this one man
can show this one boy
in this particular moment
his grandpa loves him
and asks nothing more
of life than to hold
this chip of star, this wisp
of light, close to his heart.

Michael Escoubas began writing poetry for publication in August of 2013, after retiring from a 48-year-career in the printing industry. He writes poetry because, early in life, his mother encouraged him. Michael, who lives in Illinois, is the author of three collections—*Light Comes Softly, Monet in Poetry and Paint, Steve Henderson in Poetry and Paint,* and his most recent, *Little Book of Devotions: Poems that Connect Nature, God, and Man.*

Laughter
by
Michael Estabrook

My mother called today
wants to pay for her funeral
in advance "so you boys don't have
to worry about it."
But I'm not sure how
one does that, who do you pay
after all she may live
another 15 years so I say
just write me a check you can trust me
$20,000 ought to cover it.
Been a long time
since I've heard her laugh so hard.

––––––––––

Michael Estabrook, a small press poet since the 1980s, says he is "always striving for greater clarity and concision and for rendering language more succinct, precise, accessible and appealing—a Sisyphean adventure for sure." Now retired after 40 years, Michael is enjoying having more time to write and to work outdoors. He has published more than 20 collections, a recent one being *The Poet's Curse, A Miscellany*. Michael lives in Massachusetts.

It's Good to Be King
by
Jose Ferrer

Everywhere I go,
there are rules I have to follow—
someone telling me what to do.
"A man's home is his castle." Ha!
I bet the guy who said that
was not in earshot of his wife.
Yes, everywhere, someone else makes the rules—
except in my garden.
There, *I* am the King and *I* make the rules.
You! Tomatoes! Stand up straight and tall!
Zucchini! Lay low and cover the ground!
Peppers, toil in the sun and produce a bit more;
anyone who doesn't produce will pay
for their sin with their life!
Weeds, you annoy me; it's off with your heads!
And bugs, you come like poachers in the night,
eating what is mine; when I catch you
I'll crush you under my thumb!
But you, my little sweet petunia—
you make me smile.
You will be the jester in my court,
in this garden—*my* garden,
where I make the rules,
I am the King and, yes,
it's good to be King.

————————

Jose Ferrer is a systems analyst in Greenville, South Carolina, who spent
many years working for Fortune 100 companies before launching his own
software development company. A creative thinker who enjoys problem
solving, helping small businesses use technology, and exploring new
technologies that can make the world a better place, Jose is also a dedicated
Master Gardener who is happiest on his tractor or teaching someone about
the magic of worm castings.

God's Chipmunk
by
Marsha Foss

Dead on the patio after a storm.
Good, I think to myself,
another bit of vermin who won't be
squirreling its nasty way into my attic.

Abram, almost four, spots the poor creature,
dismayed that I am carrying a shovel
and heading toward the trash can.
"Mormor," he gasps, "you can't just throw him away."
I stop. I guess I really can't. Not now.

So we gather our gloves and our spades,
dig a proper grave beside the flowers,
and say a few kind words.
"God loves you, little chipmunk," Abram intones.
Walking up from the garden, he shouts out to neighbor Elisabeth,
"We had to bury him. He was struck by lightning!"

Well, maybe he was,
or maybe he fell from the wall in the wind last night
or maybe one of Elisabeth's many cats killed him.
Whatever the reason,
we know that the God of Abram loves
even you, little chipmunk.

Marsha Foss, a retired educator, spends her time between her two favorite
states, Maryland and Minnesota. When in St. Paul, she enjoys being
connected to that area's vibrant writing community. Marsha's work has
been published in numerous places, and she has been nominated for a
Pushcart Prize. An added joy is living near two young grandsons.

Disobedience
by
Gretchen Friel

As a child I begged
for buttermilk,
the creamy texture
promising to be
vanilla milkshake.
My father enjoyed it so,
a chaser for his liverwurst on rye,
brown mustard and raw onions.
So much of his joy
requiring grown-up taste.
My mother gave me peanut butter
on squishy white bread,
mini mountains of sugar-boiled fruit
dotting the middle of my sandwich.
Preacher-like,
she rationed potato chips,
insisted on whole milk
to wash them down.
Later, I'd sneak to the fridge
with my jam glass,
Tom and Jerry cheering me on,
spend all I dared
with mystical confidence
to taste the forbidden sample.
Tears welling in my eyes,
I spat sour milk and
disappointment
into the sink,
mother's eyebrows
sympathetically raised
behind the open fridge door.
"Buttermilk! Blah!"

Gretchen Friel teaches English, German, and creative writing to high
school students in Northern Illinois, where she lives with her husband.
They have five adult children between them, and five grandchildren. Most
recently, Gretchen has written a poetic memoir and is sharing one poem at
a time on her Instagram site: @rescuedpoeticmemoir.

Right on Red
by
Sarah Gilbert

I'm sitting at a stoplight
behind a white-haired woman
in a maroon sedan.
She's missing her chance
to turn right on red
while the cross traffic
has a left arrow.
Her fluffy head turns
left right left right
but the car idles.
I'm running a little late.
The two cars that
nipped around her
before the intersection
recede into the distance
but I'm thinking about my mom
who doesn't drive anymore
and about my dad
whom nobody passed
even in the days
of towing the sailboat to the cottage
five kids piled in the station wagon
no seatbelts
and I'm thinking about my husband
whose blood pressure would be
unhealthily high by now
and I'm blessing
this old lady
though hoping
that at the next corner
she'll go one way
and I another.

Sarah Gilbert is the author of one chapbook, *Tendril: Living with Lynch Syndrome*. She writes, weaves, reads, gardens, walks, volunteers, and nestles with her family and cats in Appleton, Wisconsin.

A Dog's Life
by
Ruth Gooley

On the far side of the park's thick lawn,
a big white dog of uncertain breed.

The kind whose head flies high,
muzzle thrust before him,
as he chases the late afternoon light
with a howl, or a growl,
or a doggy version of a purr.

The kind that tastes the day
with a long felt-tipped tongue and a slurp,
the bulb of a nose quivering
at the scent of a rabbit, someone's lunch,
a gopher hidden in a hole.

The kind with long-lashed eyes
that scan passersby with longing for a pet, or a handout.
The kind that leaps after a squirrel,
darts after a shadow on the ground,
examines an airplane as it dissolves into fog.

The kind that searches in a branch for a wren,
nuzzles into rocks for a lizard,
throws himself at a passing pug,
raises his head to his master's hand
for a caress and some kibble.

This is the kind of dog I saw,
on the far side of the park,
at the corner of Westwood and Wilshire.
This is the dog I saw and adopted,
that long ago day at the park.

———————

Ruth Gooley is the author of a chapbook, *Living in Nature* (July 2018), and has published poems in a variety of journals and online publications. She makes her home in a cabin in the Santa Monica mountains, where she lives in harmony with the abundance of nature there.

What I Want and What I Can Have
by
Jeanie Greensfelder

After dinner, I try to digest
kale and cauliflower in my longing
to live longer, and a root-beer float
in case my world ends tomorrow.

I play the gamble game with exercise
and diet, reminded daily by obituaries
featuring people younger than me:
the impossible becoming likely.

I want to go out full, embraced by my life,
the grand quilt of being here. Yet memories
are remnants and come one patch at a time.
And like moments, most fade unnoticed.

After a storm, I take a walk.
At the jasmine vine by my front door,
a raindrop, suspended on a stem, stops me.
What I want, what I can have, merge.

———————

Jeanie Greensfelder is the author of three poetry collections. A
psychologist, she seeks to understand herself and others on this shared
journey filled, as Joseph Campbell said, *"with sorrowful joys and joyful sorrows."*
Jeanie lives in San Luis Obispo, California, where she volunteers as a
bereavement counselor and where she served as the 2017-18 Poet Laureate
for that city. Learn more about her at jeaniegreensfelder.com.

Deer
by
Bill Griffin

Omigosh oh snap
oh horrors I heard it
so close too close
and way too big
might be one of those
Little Wolves I'll bet
there are two
no ten a whole pack
oh God I just know
they bite
I
must
do
as
Ma
ma
said
stand
per
fect
ly
still
un
til
he
turns
a
way
then
run
like
Oh heck, it's only
you, and you've been
looking at me
all day long
and haven't even
seen me
once.

———————

Bill Griffin is a family physician in rural North Carolina. The author of six collections, his poems have appeared in many regional and national journals. For a week in 2012, Bill lived at the NC Zoological Park in Asheboro as Poet-in-Residence; this poem was a result of that experience and is on permanent display there. Learn more about Bill at https://griffinpoetry.com/.

Vulnerable
by
Tony Gruenewald

I'd not noticed
the word had gone on vacation,
slipping off unannounced
to some uncharted precinct
of my brain with which
I'm not at all familiar.

I only realized it
was away while involved
in a conversation which
could not continue
without its participation.

A few hours later,
after a cheap flight back
from the Isle of Aphasia,
it unpacked its overnight bag
and asked,
Did you miss me?

———————

Tony Gruenewald lives in New Jersey and works as an archivist for major media companies in New York. He's the author of one book, *The Secret History of New Jersey,* and his poems have appeared in numerous journals and publications. Tony claims to be "an unrepentant baseball geek;" he also enjoys hiking and road trips. Learn more about him at www.tonygruenewald.com.

Chant of the Computer-Weary
by
Mary Lee Hahn

update
download
Internet
code

password
fire wire
USB
load

keyboard
network
charger cord
mouse

sunshine
fresh air
out of the
house

Mary Lee Hahn lives in Columbus, Ohio, and has taught fourth- and fifth-graders for almost 40 years. She is the author of *Reconsidering Read-Aloud* and has had poems published in nearly a dozen anthologies.

-

Late for the Gratitude Meeting
by
Paul Hostovsky

The guy in front of me in traffic
is letting everyone in,
waving at the cars like a policeman
or a pope—
and I really have no patience for all
the indulgence
and magnanimity at my expense

because I'm late for the gratitude meeting,
which is only an hour long.
And if I miss the first ten minutes
of silent meditation I'm going to scream,
because it's my favorite part and because
it helps me remember to breathe.
And I'm going to throttle this guy

if he doesn't stop deferring
to all of the trundling humanity
turning left onto Main
at this intersection where I'm fuming,
not feeling the love,
not feeling the gratitude,
feeling only resentment and disdain

because I have the right of way.
Would you rather be right
or have peace? Let go, I can hear them say
at the gratitude meeting three blocks away,
striking the rim of the Tibetan singing bowl,
which begins vibrating,
and keeps on vibrating,
like this steering wheel I can't stop clenching.

————————

Paul Hostovsky is the author of 12 books of poetry and his award-winning poems have been widely published. Paul makes his living in Boston as a sign language interpreter and Braille instructor. Learn more about him at www.paulhostovsky.com.

Windshield Wipers
by
Susan A. Hyde

Back and forth they swipe and wipe,
brushing off the rain.
On and on they never pause
clearing off the panes.

Push one button and they're on,
flicking fog and rain.
Oh, to have the same within,
wipers for my brain.

───────────

Susan A. Hyde is a student, teacher, mother, and grandmother who has
spent her life trying to figure out what she wants to do. After years of trying
this and that, she stumbled into a poetry class led by a remarkable teacher
and, after a year under his guidance, glimpsed how poetry could work or be
a dud. Finally dipping pen in ink (metaphorically) after all this time, Susan
has begun to decide what she thinks about the world and her way within it,
exploring topics ranging from her feral cat to international politics. Poetry is
now her way to put life in nutshells. Susan, the author of *A Listing Wind*,
lives in Dallas, Texas.

Hiding Place
by
C. F. Kelly

What's happened to my coffee cup?
I search each room; I'll not give up—
I know I put it someplace near;
so how could it just disappear?
I stomp and stew! I rant and rave!
Who hid it in the microwave?

Cornelius Farrell Kelly lives with his wife in Pinedale, Wyoming, in a house they built with the help of their children at an altitude of 7300 feet above sea level. The author of eight chapbooks, he writes a rhyming couplet every morning and posts it on his Facebook page. Cork is a competitive senior swimmer (he says he frequently gets ideas for a poem while swimming) and participated in the National Games in 2019 in Albuquerque, New Mexico.

Love Blooms
by
Janet Leahy

Jeremiah presses the flowers into my hand
and says *I love you*
there are at least a dozen
maybe thirteen exquisite blooms

We have known each other
less than a year
but long enough to fall in love

He is charming
lively and entertaining
honest with his emotions
enthusiastic about new adventures

Do you like them he asks
eyes dancing with delight
Oh yes
thank you I say
giving him a hug

I can get more he replies
Teacher
there's a million out there
I can pick more
He holds up his hands
yellow from the yellow blooms

Tomorrow I say
bring some tomorrow

Janet Leahy views poetry as a shelter from the storm of noise that
bombards us. She appreciates the way the rhythms of poetry cross borders
and stir connections between diverse groups. Her garden grows—not
always as planned—but always with splashes of color and vines of morning
glory and sweet pea. Janet is a member of the Wisconsin Fellowship of
Poetry and works with critique groups in the Milwaukee-Waukesha area;
her work has been featured in anthologies, literary journals, and online. She
has published two collections of poetry and is currently working on a third.

I Meant to Do My Work Today
by
Richard Le Gallienne

I meant to do my work today—
  But a brown bird sang in the apple tree,
And a butterfly flitted across the field,
  And all the leaves were calling me.

And the wind went sighing over the land,
  Tossing the grasses to and fro,
And a rainbow held out its shining hand—
  So what could I do but laugh and go?

———————

Richard Le Gallienne (1866 - 1947) was born in Liverpool, England. A contemporary of Oscar Wilde and W. B. Yeats, he was widely published but tended to be more of a romantic than his counterparts. He moved to the U.S. in 1903, hoping to breathe new life into his writing career, but his continued preference for sentimental styling kept him out of sync with American tastes of that time. He moved to Paris in 1927 and began writing a weekly column for the *New York Sun*, which was a perfect venue for his romantic style of writing. A compilation of some of those columns won Le Gallienne an award for "best book about France by a foreigner." In the course of his life, Le Gallienne wrote nearly ninety books and innumerable articles.

The Guys Who Work Inside My Head
by
Tamara Madison

I don't know their names or gender
or whether they even have a gender.
I forget they're even there like I forget
a name, a fact, a necessary detail.
I only have to wonder aloud and then
move on to another thought when I feel
a little tap on my shoulder or sense
the presence of a calm being behind me
and there he is, or she, or it, handing me
a folder wrapped in a metaphor containing
the datum I couldn't bring to mind
that short time ago. Then I can go on living,
assured that my mind still works, that the guys
in there have not run off to serve a younger
or more facile mind, that they're with me still
in their khaki pants, buttoned-down shirts
and wire-rimmed glasses, poised to run
to the file box where they know just where
to find my username and password, the place
where we took that photo with the sea crashing
behind us, or the name of that actor, you know,
the guy who starred in that movie with that
actress, you know, the pretty one with the wide
smile and the shining teeth.

———————

Tamara Madison is the author of the chapbook, *The Belly Remembers*, and two full-length volumes of poetry, *Wild Domestic* and *Moraine*. A former teacher of English and French in a Los Angeles high school, she is also a dog lover, a swimmer, and a native Californian who has lived in many different places in the U.S. and abroad. Tamara lives in Los Alamitos, California.

Grocery Checkout
by
Robert Manchester

Candy.
Racks of it
within his grasp.

No!
But, Mom?

She moves ahead
emptying her cart.

Gum.
Hey, I
said no!

He turns to see
An older face.
She smiles.
Remembering.

Robert Manchester lives in New Hampshire, surrounded by leafy trees, stone walls, memories of Robert Frost, and several *living* poetry legends. He's been writing and publishing poems for 50+ years. Robert belongs to the John Hay Poetry Group in Newbury, New Hampshire.

Melinda Cleans My Teeth
by
Charlotte Mandel

Intent blue eyes
of prairie skies—
white coat and denim jeans—
Her fingers click
with a silver pick
exploring before she cleans—
A musical straw
gobbles in my jaw
like a flute with dancing beans—
While toot' by toot'
'round each tingling root
a bladelet intervenes—
Now a powerbrush
circles in a rush,
toboggan-fast careens—
To the orange taste
of a sandy paste
rubbed in by tambourines—
The pirouette
of a pistol jet
splashes in serpentines—
Swirled in spit
the scouring grit
is sluiced and sucked from the scene—
And my teeth applaud
with a smile as broad
as diamond mezzanines.

———————

Charlotte Mandel spent the first half of her life as a suburban wife and
mother. In her mid-forties, she discovered a love for poetry and is now the
author of 11 books. Charlotte's work has earned her numerous fellowships,
residencies, and awards—including the 2012 New Jersey Poet's Prize and a
Lifetime Achievement Award from Brooklyn College. Now retired after
several years teaching poetry writing at Barnard College Center for Research
on Women, Charlotte lives in New Jersey. Learn more about her
at www.charlottemandel.com.

Summer
by
William Marr

To say that your smile
lights up the whole garden
is of course an exaggeration

but I did indeed see
a flower bloom
at your approach

William Marr came to America from Taiwan in 1961. With a master's degree in mechanical engineering and a PhD in nuclear engineering, he worked in energy research for 27 years before retiring to focus on his true passions—poetry and art. William is the author of two books of essays, several books of poetry translations, and 23 volumes of poetry. His work has been translated into more than ten languages and appears in high school and college textbooks in Taiwan, China, England, and Germany. In 2018, William received a lifetime achievement award from the International Board of Examiners of Edizioni Universum and the Albert Nelson Marquis Lifetime Achievement Award from the Marquis Who's Who Publications Board. In 2019, he received the 60th Literary Award from Taiwan's Chinese Literature and Art Association. William lives with his wife in a suburb of Chicago, Illinois.

Procrastinator's Plight
by
Lauren McBride

"I've put this off too long," I sigh,
surveying the chaos before me.
With broom and duster in my hand
I can't get past the doorway!

One shoe I spy, and my best shirt
where dust bunnies swirl in place.
Pop cans, socks, old magazines—
I'm starting to clear a space.

I venture a step and hear a crunch,
look down to find my glasses
lying crushed beneath a broken plate
caked with something like molasses.

The TV sits collecting dust—
remote's been lost for months.
As for walking over to turn it on?
Tried that exactly once:

Got tangled in a towel,
smacked my head against the wall.
Braced myself for impact—
dirty laundry broke my fall.

Just found the missing car keys,
and a cockroach, thankfully dead.
Almost there, I can see it now.
I've finally found my bed!

Lauren McBride finds inspiration in faith, family, nature, science, and
membership in the Science Fiction & Fantasy Poetry Association (SFPA).
Nominated for various awards, her work has appeared internationally in
speculative and mainstream publications for adults and young adults.
Lauren lives in Texas, where she enjoys swimming, gardening, baking,
reading, writing, and knitting scarves for troops.

The Divorce
by
Janet McCann

My printer has divorced
my computer.
There was a little ceremony
last week after midnight.
Some clicking and a whine of separation.

Now my printer prints randomly,
wakes me from slumber
with industrious humming
and rattle of snatched paper.
Here come some Venn diagrams
and a page of Portuguese.

Of course I could unplug it
or even take a hammer to it
but I like the messages.

It invites me to random events,
emits puppies and kittens,
warns me about exotic diseases.
I'm hoping it will finish up the poems
I abandoned years ago
for lack of interest.

Cut off from its source and reason
I thought it would surely die,
yet I keep watching it from the margin
of my vision eagerly, expectantly.

———————

Janet McCann has been teaching creative writing and other vices to Aggies
at Texas A&M for more than 50 years. Her award-winning work is widely
published in several genres, and she was honored with a fellowship from
the National Endowment for the Arts. Janet lives in College Station, Texas,
where she worries about feral cats and other beings who are overlooked or
abused.

Road Work
by
Tom Montag

Road crew—
The work takes
one man.

The watching,
three.

Tom Montag was raised on an Iowa farm, but now lives in Wisconsin.
Retired from a career in the printing industry, he is the author of several
books of poetry as well as several books of prose. He's also a songwriter
and plays bass, as often as he can. For many years, Tom has taught creative
nonfiction and poetry at The Mill: A Place for Writers, in Appleton,
Wisconsin. His work has appeared in numerous literary magazines and one
of his poems is on permanent display in Milwaukee's Convention Center.
Learn more about him at www.middlewesterner.com.

Hells Angels
by
Julie L. Moore

Ablaze with buzz like the motors that drone
as cycles pass by,

bumblebees, in their striped jackets,
black helmets, and snug gloves,

cruise through the coreopsis
while their pollen passengers hug them tight.

And when my water splashes the blooms,
they rev their engines and peel out—

sun soaking their necks,
wind flying in their faces—

and they guzzle like Hells Angels
the nectar of an open road.

Julie L. Moore believes that writing poetry is as vital as seeking justice,
embracing beauty, and emulating goodness. Author of four poetry
collections, Julie's work has appeared in many literary publications and
anthologies. She lives in Indiana, where she is an Associate Professor of
English and the Writing Center director at Taylor University. Learn more
about Julie at www.julielmoore.com.

Vanilla as Vinyl
by
Mike Orlock

I'm an analog man in a digital world.
I'm relevant as vinyl.
I'm so lost in cyberspace
even a Google search can't find me.

I suspect . . . no, I *know*
my smart phone is smarter
than I. It asks me
questions I can't answer,
takes me places
I'm too stupid to exit.
I have to ask my grandchildren
to help me figure out
what I've done,
where I've gone,
how I got there,
even who I am
in this brave new world
of compact, candy-colored
super-conductivity.

If I were a color,
I'd be beige.
If I were a flavor,
I'd be very vanilla.

Mike Orlock is a retired high school English and American History teacher who divides his time between the Chicago suburbs and a vacation home in Sturgeon Bay, Wisconsin. He has been married for 46 years to his high school sweetheart and greatly enjoys being grandfather to five beautiful granddaughters who keep him, he says, "jumping like a frog on a hot skillet." Mike's short stories, poems, and reviews have appeared in a variety of publications and he is the author of three books. He is currently serving a two-year appointment as Poet Laureate of Door County, Wisconsin.

Small Town
by
Alice N. Persons

A caller complained because a wrecker stopped on County Road because ducks were crossing the road on June 12. Then on June 14 police controlled traffic while a snapping turtle crossed Huston Road.

— from Police Notes, Gorham, Maine, July 2015

This is why I live in my small Maine town,
a place where the hip coffee place only lasted a year,
where citizens show up to city council and committee meetings
to passionately debate zoning changes, fireworks ordinances, potholes.
If you email or call your town officials, they get back to you.
There's rarely a line at City Hall to renew your dog license
or register your car.
The mailman made friends with my dog long ago.
The neighbors notice anything new in my yard.
And somewhere on a fine summer day, on his way to pick up a dead car,
the driver of a big wrecker caps his coffee and stops
in the middle of a busy road
so some heedless ducks can waddle importantly across.

———————

Alice N. Persons is the editor and publisher of Moon Pie Press, which publishes work by poets from all over the country and now has more than a hundred books in its catalog. Author of five collections herself, Alice lives in Westbrook, Maine with two cats and a dog, all rescues. She serves on the board of the Animal Refuge League of Greater Portland and enjoys painting, walking her dog, holidays, travel, baking, and Maine in all seasons.

The Only Thing I Want
by
Marcia J. Pradzinski

is the weather forecast
five minutes on the computer
I chase the arrow
as it sets me sliding then sludging
through a bog of e-mails
I take a break on Facebook
where I float
for minutes on end
when I remember a message
I've forgotten to send
the arrow glides toward my account
then jumps flies away and hits
a pop-up of recipes
I grip the mouse
but the cursor soars
to a sale of shoes handbags
cookware cocktail attire
hits a link singing
You're today's winner
while flashing neon red
then tracks a trail back
and forth here and there
dragging me from
a five-minute plan
to check the weather
through an hour of wandering
computer mouse leading the way
and I still don't know
if it's going to rain.

Marcia J. Pradzinski is a Chicago native who now lives in Skokie, Illinois.
Having taught English in the International Teaching Assistants program in
Chicago for many years, Marcia has always loved words in their many
contexts: in print, in songs, and in foreign languages such as Polish and
Ukrainian, which she heard spoken while growing up. The author of *Left
Behind*, Marcia's poems have been featured in anthologies and in many print
and online journals. She gives credit to her poet colleagues for helping her
stay productive and accountable.

Texting
by
Anita S. Pulier

Consider giving up ings
vowels complex sentences
abandoning adjectives
nothing left to parse
spin a weave of
silent sound bytes
paperless symbols
unrestrained by punctuation
string word remnants together
until naked towers of
abbreviations slang and symbols
strip bare the raw meat of language
once the essence
of human experience
spit out the masticated pulp
decorate with a smiley face
not all that much to lol about

Anita S. Pulier is a retired attorney who traded legal writing for poetry. She and her husband divide their time between their native New York City and Los Angeles, where their children and grandchildren live. They enjoy daily hikes in either NYC parks or the Santa Monica Mountains. Author of three chapbooks and two full-length collections of poetry, Anita is active in the Southern California poetry community and her work has appeared in many journals and anthologies. Learn more about her at http://psymeet.com/anitaspulier/main/index.php.

Sprig Has Cub
by
Edwin C. Ranck

Sprig, Sprig—Oh lovely Sprig!
Oh, hast thou cub to stay?
Add wilt the little birdies sig
Throughout the livelog day?
What bessage dost thou brig to be,
Fair Lady of by dreabs—
Dost whisper of the babblig brook
Ad fishig poles ad streabs?
Those happy days have cub agaid,
The sweetest of the year,
Whed bad cad raise ad appetite
Ad wholesub thirst for beer.
I've often thought I'd wudder, Sprig,
Of how the lily grows,
But the thig that's botherig be dow
Is how to sprig dew clothes.
Sprig, Sprig—Oh lovely Sprig!
By thoughts are all of you
I saw a robid yesterday—
How strange it seebs—ad dew!
I've got a dreadful cold, Fair Sprig,
Or else I'd sig to thee
Ad air frob Beddelssohd, perhaps,
Or "The Shade of the Old Apple Tree."

———————

Edwin Carty Ranck (1879 - 1957) was born in in Lexington, Kentucky. His
father was a writer and newspaper editor. After attending Harvard, Edwin
followed in his father's footsteps and became a journalist, writing at one
point for the *New York Times*.

The Roadside Assistance Prayer
by
Susan Rooke

Let us give thanks today
for one of the Lord's great blessings,
the Roadside Assistance program,
the guardian angel
of the hapless driver
who cannot change a tire,
like me,
or whose rear differential
cracks like an unwrapped pipe in January,
like mine.

Let us give praise
for that tow truck,
the sight of which
brings a lump squeezing
to the throat every time,
the body so broad and capable,
the flat bed like folded wings,
flanks glistening with fiery script
like the word of the Almighty
emblazoned on a tablet, thus:

Jerry's
Southside
A-1.

Amen.

———————

Susan Rooke and her husband live surrounded by pampered black cows,
two grumpy donkeys, and amazing birdlife in the countryside of Central
Texas. Susan writes fiction as well as poetry and is the author of the first
two books in a fantasy series, *The Space Between* and *The Realm Below*.
Periodically she blogs about real life, food, and cocktails
at http://susanrooke.net.

Art Project
by
Sarah Russell

Supplies:
Construction paper
Scissors with blunt ends
Crayons
One grandchild

Directions:
Fold the paper down the middle
Draw an ear shape up to the fold
Cut around the ear shape

Results:
The ear becomes a heart
Surprise
Giggles
Hugs

Clean-up:
Nope
Just paper hearts flying
everywhere

———————

Sarah Russell recently moved, with her husband and curly dog, from
Pennsylvania to Colorado to be near her children and grandchildren.
Author of *I Lost Summer Somewhere* and *Today and Other Seasons*, her poetry
has been published in a variety of online and print publications. Learn more
about Sarah at www.SarahRussellPoetry.net.

Robo Calls
by
Signe Eklund Schaefer

The phone rings,
a recorded voice ominously commands,
Call this number
the IRS is filing a lawsuit against you.
My husband hangs up laughing,
but as we speak of the trickery
behind this cruel tape
the phone rings again.
I take it this time:
Congratulations, you've been selected
for a free cruise to the Bahamas.
Hanging up once more
I wonder aloud
if the trip is to be scheduled before
or after the arrival of the IRS.

———————

Signe Eklund Schaefer's articles and poems have appeared in several anthologies and journals and she is the author of four books, most recently, *I Give You My Word - Women's Letters as Life Support, 1973-1987.* Signe has lived and taught in many different countries, always pondering the mysteries of human life and development. Now retired, she has rediscovered the joy of inviting poems to express daily moments and memories. Signe lives in western Massachusetts with her husband of more than 50 years.

The Street That Doesn't Need Realtors
by
Shoshauna Shy

stretches one block and ends at a park
High school grads leave for distant adventures
then return once they become moms and dads

Emails spin out to take cookie sandwich orders
before bike runs are made to Trader Joe's

A newsletter announces whose strawberries are ripe
and asks who wants to split an order of birch trees

Every fifth June a party is held for anybody who ever
lived on this street and librarians from lush Colorado
valleys and investment bankers who roam oceans in yachts

return to reminisce about smoking Marlboros
and playing Spin-the-Bottle with the Flossy twins
and who scared Whitman's dogs by lighting firecrackers

When the lilacs start to bloom tables show up on porches
Ironing boards are propped in the thumbprint front yards
and barbecue suppers get grilled at the curb

You should see all the sofas out there

––––––––––

Shoshauna Shy began writing at the age of eight on a manual Olivetti. The author of five poetry collections, she usually gets ideas for new poems while stuck doing something else. Not a monogamous writer, she's usually working on 7-11 pieces at one time, and flash fiction is also in the mix. A cat care business affords Shoshauna plenty of writing time in other peoples' quiet houses. Learn more about her at
https://www.PoetryJumpsOfftheShelf.com.

Harvest Night
by
Richard Swanson

Another disastrous year, he laughs.

April: Pepper seedlings left outside, shot through with frost.
May: Thriving tomato sprouts scorched by sudden heat.
Rare Swiss chard mistaken for weeds, flung to the compost.

June and July: everything under- or over-watered,
aphids viewed as benign till almost too late.

That night, that night in August
when he left the gate ajar, and the roaming rabbits
moved in for a leveling gourmet marathon –
what a story, that one, one for the gardening ages.

All alone, out on his porch, he considers:
How bumbling and unprofitable my efforts.
How small and inept I am,
but we have had a summer adventure,
these earthy things and I.

In the softened light of a candle he is pouring champagne
and toasting, tipping the flute's edge to the season past
and the last of his yield, on his plate:

the lone sweet corn ear, its twenty-five kernels gleaming,
the handful of bush beans, tenderly anorexic,
the mini-eggplant that might have graced a starlet's ear.

Richard Swanson is a retired English teacher in Madison, Wisconsin.
Author of two chapbooks and three full-length poetry collections, his
poems are noted for their humor and humanity and often focus on popular
culture. Besides writing, Richard enjoys good books, gardening, cooking,
and artisan woodworking.

Final Wishes
by
Carroll S. Taylor

When I am gone
don't put me in a box
Set my soul free
Cremate my body
Mix my ashes
with dollar store glitter
Dance around a fire
on a moonlit night
and toss me in the air
Watch me sparkle
one more time

———————

Carroll S. Taylor and her husband live in Hiawassee, Georgia. A retired educator, she is the author of two young adult novels, *Chinaberry Summer* and *Chinaberry Summer: On the Other Side*. She is also the author of a new children's book, *Feannag the Crow,* which teaches children how important it is to have friends. Carroll's novels emphasize generational storytelling and anti-bullying, and her stories and poems reflect her affection for reptiles, amphibians, spiders, and other critters. Learn more about her at chinaberrysummer.com.

Cover the Mirror, Joe
by
Phyllis Wax.

I blow in the door—
Wild Woman of the East
side of town—hair
flying in all directions.

*I've come for you to tame
the beast.* I fall into the chair
and turn my back on the mirror.
I can't bear to look. I surrender

to the strait-jacket cape
that surrounds me, keeps my hands
away from my hair so I won't
tear it out.

Joe quietly assesses
the mess: walks to my left side,
passes in front of me and squints
at the right side, circles to the back,
lifts clumps and strands checking
lengths, tests strength of curls,
the natural tendency to wave
and then wave back.

To him I am simply
an untended forsythia.
He grabs his shears,
starts to prune.

———————

Phyllis Wax writes in Milwaukee, Wisconsin on a bluff overlooking Lake
Michigan. From her office window, she watches the seasons change, the
migrating birds which use the lake as their GPS, and an amazing variety of
wildlife which manages to thrive in the city. Widely published both online
and in print, Phyllis has read her poetry on the radio, in coffee shops, in
libraries and bars. Her work has been exhibited with art quilts and weavings
in a variety of venues within Wisconsin as part of four poet/fiber artist
collaborations.

Credits

For previously copyrighted and/or previously published poems:

"A Drawer Filled to Overflowing," by Wendy Morton, is from *Shadowcatcher* (Ekstasis Editions, 2005)

"Beach Reverie," by Dorothy K. Fletcher, is from *Zen Fishing and Other Southern Pleasures* (Ocean Publishing, 2005)

"Begin with the Faucet", by Christine Swanberg, is from *Wild Fruition: Sonnets, Spells, and Other Incantations* (Puddin'head Press, 2017).

"Cautionary," by Dana Wildsmith, is from *Our Bodies Remember* (Sow's Ear Press, 1999)

"Chaperone," by Kay Day, is from *A Poetry Break* (Ocean Publishing, 2004)

"Deer," by Bill Griffin, is from *Snake Den Ridge, A Bestiary* (March Street Press, 2008)

"Everything About Egypt," by Edwin Romond, is from *Dream Teaching* (Grayson Books, 2004)

"Forty Pounds of Moorparks," by Grace Hughes Chappell, is from *Ten Mile Creek Almanac* (Finishing Line Press, 2019)

"Funeral Arrangements," by Barbara Eknoian, is from *Jerkumstances* (Pearl Editions, 2003)

"Harvest Night," by Richard Swanson, is from *Not Quite Eden* (Fireweed Press, 2010)

"Hells Angels," by Julie L. Moore, first appeared in *Particular Scandals: A Book of Poems*; reprinted with permission by Wipf & Stock Publishers, https://wipfandstock.com/9781620327883/particular-scandals/

"Hiding Place," by C. F. Kelly, is from *Collected Poems* (CreateSpace, 2016)

"Horseplay," by George Bilgere, is from *Blood Pages* (University of Pittsburgh Press, 2018)

"In Praise of Doorsteps," by Janice Canerdy, first appeared in the Fall 2012 contest-edition anthology of the Mississippi Poetry Society

"In the Shade of the Tractor's Wheel," by Peter Christensen, is from *Oona River Poems* (Thistledown Press, 2019)

"LuRay Love", by Jan Chronister, is from *Caught Between Coasts: Collected Poems 1989-2018* (Clover Valley Press, 2018)

"My Daughter at the Age of Reason," by David Alpaugh, is from *Heavy Lifting* (Alehouse Press, 2007)

"Ordinary Life," by Barbara Crooker, is from *Barbara Crooker: Selected Poems* (FutureCycle Press, 2015)

"Small Town," by Alice N. Persons, is from *Fancy Meeting You Here* (Moon Pie Press, 2015)

"Summer," by William Marr, is from *Between Heaven and Earth* (PublishAmerica, 2010)

"Texting," by Anita S. Pulier, is from *The Butcher's Diamond* (Finishing Line Press, 2018)

"The Feeling of Earth on My Fingertips," by Barbara Quick, is from *The Light on Sifnos* (Blue Light Press, 2021)

"Together," by Arlene Gay Levine, is from *Gratitude Prayers* (Andrews McMeel, 2013)

"Vulnerable," by Tony Gruenewald, is from *The Secret History of New Jersey* (Northwind Publishing, 2009)

"What I Want and What I Can Have," by Jeanie Greensfelder, is from *I Got What I Came For* (Penciled In, 2017)

"Where You'll Find Me," by Gail Comorat, is from *Walking the Sunken Boards* (Pond Tree Press, 2019)

"Whispers from a Bench Along the Trail", by Sara Sarna, is from *Whispers from a Bench* (Independently published, 2020)

Ingram Content Group UK Ltd.
Milton Keynes UK
UKHW02195008B0523
421401UK00015B/921

9 781955 581097